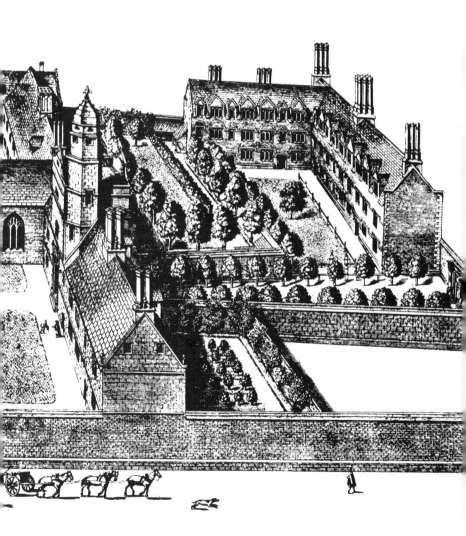

John Pory / 1572–1636

John Pory / 1572–1636

The Life and Letters
of a Man of Many Parts

by William S. Powell

Letters and Other Minor Writings
Microfiche Supplement

The University of North Carolina Press
Chapel Hill

Copyright © 1977 by
The University of North Carolina Press
All rights reserved
Manufactured in the United States of America
Clothbound biography, ISBN 0-8078-1270-6
Microfiche letters, ISBN 0-8078-1271-4
Library of Congress Catalog Card Number 75-45074

Library of Congress Cataloging in Publication Data

Powell, William Stevens, 1919–
  John Pory, 1572–1636: the life and letters of a man of many parts.

  Bibliography: p.
  Includes index.
  1. Pory, John, 1572–1636.
DA378.P6P68   975.5'01'0924 [B]   75-45074
ISBN 0-8078-1270-6

11-21-77

NOV 28 1977

For VIRGINIA

Contents ∾∾

Illustrations ∾∾

Following page 138

Acknowledgments ∾

By its very nature a work of this sort is necessarily the product of generous cooperation by many people. Scattered information about obscure characters of long ago simply cannot be discovered nor, especially in the case of a newsletter, vague illusions tracked down in any logical way. For assistance in locating material and in identifying many people, places, and events, and for guidance in transcribing several difficult passages in some of the letters I am indebted to scholars on both sides of the Atlantic. My debt is especially large to Mr. G. D. Bark, Newark, Nottinghamshire; Professors Stephen B. Baxter, Fred Behrends, and Gillian Cell of the University of North Carolina; Professor Richard Beale Davis of the University of Tennessee; the Honorable Richard de Grey, Thetford, Norfolk; Miss Joan M. Kennedy, Norfolk and Norwich Record Office, Norwich; Professor R. A. McKinley, Leicester University; and Mr. R. J. Olney, Lincolnshire Archives Office. Professor Leo M. Kaiser, Loyola University of Chicago, was generous to me as he has been to countless others in identifying and translating Latin quotations. Professor David B. Quinn, Liverpool University, not only encouraged me to persist in my search for information but also advised me on many obscure points.

Without the friendly and helpful assistance and advice of the staffs of numerous libraries and archives I might have been obliged to spend many more years than I already have on this book. For very special favors which I shall always recall with pleasure as I turn these pages, I must mention members of the staff, known and unknown by name to me, at the Library of Congress, the Huntington Library, the New York Public Library, the Bodleian Library, the British Library, the Public Record Office, and the Institute of Historical Research at the University of London. To my friends of long standing at the University of North Carolina, Duke University, and Yale University libraries I have already often expressed my appreciation but do so again with sincerity.

To Paul Wyche, Lana Stocks, and Sanford Boswell, student assistants, excellent typists, and by now more knowledgeable in matters of the seventeenth century than they ever expected to be, my thanks for their accuracy and diligence on my behalf. To Linda U. Stephenson, Pat Maynor, and Secily Jones of the staff of the History Department of the University of North Carolina, goes my special appreciation for preparing the final version for the press.

Credit lines beneath the illustrations identify the individuals and institutions to whom my sincere thanks go for permitting me to use copies of material in their possession.

For permission to publish the original manuscript letters in their care I am grateful to the Trustees of the British Library; to the Controller of H. M. Stationery Office with respect to Crown-copyright records in the Public Record Office; to the Deputy Keeper of the Old Library, Magdalene College, Cambridge; to the Duke of Buccleuch and Queensberry, K.T., G.C.V.O.; to the John Carter Brown Library, Brown University; and to the Manuscript Division, The New York Public Library, Astor, Lennox and Tilden Foundations.

For research grants which made possible two of my four trips to England in search of the sometimes elusive John Pory, I am grateful to the Institute of Early American History and Culture, Williamsburg, Virginia; and to the Guggenheim Foundation.

Finally, yet in truth foremost, gratitude beyond expression to my most capable assistant in all of this, Virginia Waldrop Powell, who has often voiced an understanding of bigamy, having been married to me and to John Pory since 14 June 1952.

WILLIAM S. POWELL

Chronology ❧

Introduction ∾∾

The years between 1572 and 1636, the lifetime of John Pory, saw many changes taking place in England. From a largely self-sufficient nation with only incidental interest in overseas expansion, England became an empire of people who took an active interest in events at home and had intellectual ties and economic relations with widely scattered regions of the world. At the beginning of Pory's life Elizabeth had been queen of England for fourteen years while more than thirty yet remained to her. James was king for the following twenty-two years, and the rest of Pory's life included the first eleven years of the ill-fated Charles's twenty-four-year reign. This period of sixty-four years represents a full lifetime in terms of years as well as accomplishments. Unlike the majority of Englishmen of his station, Pory traveled widely on the Continent and in the Middle East as well to the New World. He was an active participant in many of the significant events of the time, a witness to many others, and above all an interested inquirer into important as well as trivial occurrences.

The death of Elizabeth in 1603 and the great concern over her successor, as the time of that certain yet dreaded event approached and passed, produced an atmosphere of considerable apprehension. Secret intrigue began well in advance of her death, and for a time many men concealed their sentiments for fear of recrimination at the hands of either friends or enemies. The peaceful arrival of Elizabeth's Scottish relative, James, calmed restless London, yet within weeks the great and would-be great were jostling each other to secure positions of power around the new king. James early demonstrated his inability to appreciate the differences between political channels in London and the more direct action in Edinburgh where he had become king as an infant in 1567. Because of the new king's demands for both money and power, he was soon locked in combat with the Commons. Members of his first parliament, of which Pory was one, refused to accede to his demands. A struggle for parliamentary supremacy ensued; the Crown resisted, and both sides engaged in excesses. The stage was set for the civil wars of 1642–48.

During Pory's childhood many remote regions of the world were explored, and fabulous, almost unbelievable, tales were brought back. The credulity of men was pushed to the limit. Great trading companies were formed, and goods of the world came into England. Sugar and spices, heretofore rare, now whetted the appetites of Englishmen for wider contact with the strange places they heard about from sailors and travelers. Explorations begun under Elizabeth resulted in colonies under James, and during the time of his son Charles these colonies grew into significant outposts of an expanding empire. Between East and West, to India in one direction and to America in the other, British ships and people moved freely in anticipation of a wonderful new life. As a trained geographer Pory both knew about and participated in many of these events.

At home old ways sometimes persisted, but there were signs of change on every hand. For careless acts, men and women might still be confined at the whim of the Crown in the many prisons of the day. Some of them died there of consumption; others, convicted on some vague charge or other, might be beheaded, while it was not entirely unknown for an unfortunate soul to be burned at the stake. People of high and low degree were murdered for money or politics or jealousy or for no apparent reason at all. John Pory was fully aware of such incidents, and he commented on them with a great deal of frankness to trusted confidants. Nevertheless this was the age of Shakespeare and Ben Jonson. John Donne preached magnificent sermons. Inigo Jones designed splendid houses, chapels, and palaces. The Tredescants laid out great gardens. The influence of the Pope was feared, and Roman Catholics in England paid dearly for what they hoped would be a little peace of mind. The Church of England still was feeling its way to a secure establishment, and as a devout Anglican Pory was ever alert to the opportunity to make a critical remark about the Church of Rome. He was acquainted with many of the literary and religious figures of the day and they exchanged civilities with each other, often mentioning one another in wide-ranging correspondence.

In these years of the seventeenth century most people were oppressed by someone in authority over them. The hierarchy was well established; yet even those near the top were not without some fear. Hardly a nobleman existed who at one time or another had not quaked in his boots in the presence of someone superior to him. A list of people of prominence who had spent time in prison while on their way up the ladder of personal success would be lengthy, and many such men and women did attain the peak of their ambition.

Prison to these people was no disgrace, and neither was bastardy. The kings' illegitimate children were known in this century as in the past, and most of them were honored. Men of high rank sometimes had children by other men's wives, and it was rare that a cuckolded husband protested. Indeed, his calm acceptance might thereby be the means of enlarging his landed estate, raising his position, or increasing his power. Nevertheless, it was during this time that the people of the country began to express their displeasure with the sexual license of the court. Puritanical attitudes had their roots in these years and they flourished and grew as the century passed. Pory was well acquainted with all of this and in many instances his letters reveal intimate details of life at court not otherwise recorded.

People far down the social scale also suffered from the oppression of their "betters," but they bore up under other adversities as well. Many were often near starvation at a time when noblemen, particularly those seeking to make favorable impressions and improve their own positions, entertained throngs at feasts that lasted for days and cost thousands of pounds that they could scarcely afford. Poor people might be turned out of their cottages for petty reasons or denied access to the royal forests for fuel or garden patches. They surely could not kill a stray deer from the park of the local manor even if it were destroying their fields. Medical care, of course, was little understood and proper attention was rare for all classes, but the poorer people suffered most. Many children died at an early age. A person living into his seventies was considered quite old, while anyone in his eighties or above was an object of considerable interest. People died of infected teeth as well as with an assortment of unidentified fevers and chills. Even the promising Prince Henry fell victim to a fever, since believed to have been typhoid. Superstition held sway at almost every turn: comets were cause for alarm about important national matters, many people were believed to have unworldly powers, and forces of nature were suspected of working for the good or evil of man as he happened to deserve at the moment. Again, Pory was a keen observer of this aspect of the times.

Despite all of this, signs of a changed world began to appear during this time. The universities were inquiring more deeply into scientific and philosophical questions. The sons of a vast rising middle class of land-owning gentry and increasingly wealthy merchants began to attend the colleges at Oxford and Cambridge. Newspapers appeared in England in the 1620s, and books began to be published in greater variety and quantity than ever before. More women were beginning to read and to write letters. Both Roman Catholic and Anglican doctrine came to be questioned; dissenting sects arose, and many of their members in due course departed for America.

The period of the reigns of these three interesting and successive "firsts"—Elizabeth I, James I, and Charles I—saw the rise of many men from moderately obscure backgrounds to positions of significance. John Pory himself must be counted among such people. His book on Africa published in 1600 brought him to the attention of a number of scholars, merchants, and men at court. Shakespeare was aware of the book and made use of information which it contained. John Donne and Ben Jonson established a friendship with him that lasted many years. As a member of Parliament from 1605 until 1611 Pory became acquainted with Sir Edwin Sandys and Sir Thomas Smyth, who were later prominent in the affairs of the Virginia colony at a time when Pory was employed in Virginia. In Parliament he also laid the foundation for lasting friendships with Sir Robert Cotton, Sir Walter Cope, and Dudley Carleton. Pory came to the attention of still others who were to call on him for service at various times in the future: Wentworth, Warwick, and Northumberland, among others. Both King James and King Charles sent him on special missions. The Privy Council found his services useful on more than one occasion as did several of the companies of merchants. For many years Pory lived in Paris, Constantinople, and Jamestown; and he passed through such diverse places as Plymouth (in New England), Sicily, Venice, and the Azores.

Pory was active in the field of journalism at the time when the native newspaper was beginning to make its appearance in England. He presided over the birth of the first American legislature. His numerous letters written during critical times of the Thirty Years' War contain interesting details not generally recorded elsewhere. As an educated, literate commoner his activities and comments during an interesting time in the history of England, America, and the Continent are unique in many respects. The sheer variety of his interests and the range of his activities and friendships make him a person worthy of note.

John Pory / 1572–1636

St. Martin's Church, Thompson, Norfolk, half a mile from the site of Butters Hall, dates from about 1300. Pory was christened here and attended services in this church as a child and young man.

1. At Home and Abroad ⌘

John Pory was born in the rural farming village of Thompson, Norfolk, somewhat less than a hundred miles north of London. He and a twin sister, Mary, of whom nothing further is known, were christened in the local parish church on 16 March 1572. There was also another sister, Anne. He was the son of William Pory, the last of his line to occupy the old family home, Butters Hall (a corruption of the older Botetourts or Botours Hall). This house was in existence by 1429 but was so altered by the 1890s as to have lost its original character. It no longer stands, but the site can be identified by cellar depressions and rubble. A Butters Hall dependency, perhaps a stable cottage, stood until 1952, although it was unoccupied after the late 1940s when World War II refugees departed. Manor court was long held at Butters Hall, and some of its records are preserved in the Norfolk Record Office in Norwich.[1]

Ancestry

Pory's father, William, may have been the one of that name who enrolled in Corpus Christi College, Cambridge, in 1551.[2] Perhaps he was also the one of this name from Norfolk who contributed £25 toward England's defense against the Spanish Armada in 1588.[3] Pory's mother apparently was a Marsham, also an old Norfolk family. The Pory family had resided here and in nearby

1. The registers of St. Martin's Parish, Thompson, were lost for about thirty years until they were discovered early in 1972 among the papers of a former rector. They are now in the care of the churchwarden. Land records concerning the Pory family at Butters Hall from 1503 until 1590, when "William Pory gent. son of Peter Pory gent." surrendered the holdings to Thomas Futter, are preserved among the Walsingham muniments in Norwich (Walsingham [Merton] Collection, Norfolk and Norwich Record Office, XIX/2, XIX/7, and XIX/8). The land continued to be identified as "of Poris" as late as 1600. Lord Walsingham of nearby Merton Hall now owns the Butters Hall site.

2. John Venn and J. A. Venn, *Alumni Cantabrigiensis* (Cambridge, England, 1922), 2:383.

3. T. C. Noble, *The Names of those Persons who Subscribed Towards the Defence of this Country at the time of the Spanish Armada, 1588, and the Amounts Each Contributed* (London, 1886), p. 44.

villages in Norfolk, Suffolk, Lincolnshire, and Northamptonshire since at least as early as 1333 and had been moderately prominent in local civic and parish affairs. The name was rare and apparently derived from *atte Pyrrie* ("at the pear tree"), which occurs at times as *atte Pury* or *atte Pory* in Norfolk and Suffolk during the Middle Ages. One Pory whose given name is not now known was graduated from the University of Cambridge in 1461 with the bachelor of canon law degree, and in 1464 he was awarded the degree of doctor of canon law. Sir John Pory was rector of Merton, adjacent to Thompson, in 1507; and Richard Poore, whose surname may have been a form of the Pory name, spent almost a year from 1584 to 1585 with Ralph Lane's colony based at Roanoke Island in the New World.

A larger branch of the Pory family lived thirty-six miles west of Thompson in the fen country of Sutton St. Edmunds, Lincolnshire, only two and a half miles north of the Cambridgeshire border. This farming and grazing country, just inside the southeastern corner of Lincolnshire, lay in an area that was then subject to flooding from the sea, but Sutton St. Edmunds, situated on a slight ridge in that very flat country, usually escaped. Here Pory men became affluent, managing 170 acres and dealing in wheat, oats, barley, rye, cattle, sheep, and other livestock.[4]

An earlier John Pory (1503–70), native of Thompson and great-uncle of the Virginia colonist, was master of Corpus Christi College, Cambridge, from 1557 until 1569 and prebendary of the collegiate church of St. Peter, Westminster, until his death. The elder Pory, for whom the younger John Pory probably was named, was reputedly very wealthy and was a personal friend of Matthew Parker, archbishop of Canterbury.[5] Almost a century later the Rev-

4. At one time the Pory property at Thompson consisted of 160 acres, but the family also enjoyed the adjacent "College land," so called from the former religious establishment there which was dissolved during the reign of Henry VIII (George Crabbe, *Some Materials for a History of the Parish of Thompson* [Norwich, England, 1892] pp. 25–40, 64, 93–94). One William Porey of Sutton St. Edmund was "a great grazier and a great dealer for cattle in the county of Lincoln" (Alan Everitt, "The Marketing of Agricultural Produce," in Joan Thirsk, ed., *The Agrarian History of England and Wales*, vol. 4, *1500–1640* [Cambridge, England, 1967], p. 518; and Joan Thirsk, *English Peasant Farming, The Agrarian History of Lincolnshire from Tudor to Recent Times* [London, 1957], pp. 8, 27, 36, 138–39).

5. The will of the elder John Pory in the Public Record Office (formerly in the Principal Probate Register at Somerset House, Lyon 23), dated 7 May 1570, made his nephew, William Pory, sole executor. Bequests were made to William as well as to nephews John, Robert, and Peter Pory, and to nieces Elizabeth Enderman, Anne Brande, and Ursula Deane (Anthony A. Wood, *Athenae Oxonienses, An Exact History of All the Writers and Bishops Who Have had Their Education in the University of Oxford* [London, 1815], 2:782).

This house was one of the outbuildings at Butters Hall, Pory's birthplace. It was demolished in 1952.

erend Dr. Robert Pory was a canon of St. Paul's, London, arch-deacon of Colchester, and rector of a parish in Essex. At this man's death on 29 November 1669 it was also reported that he was wealthy.[6] The arms borne by the branch of the family to which the younger John Pory belonged was described as "Sable guttée d'eau a saltire Or."[7] Through Temperance Flowerdew, his first cousin and wife of Sir George Yeardley, his relationship has been established with John Stanley of Scottow, Norfolk (a member of the family now represented by the Earls of Derby), and with the Marsham family, also of Norfolk (now represented by the Earls of Romney).[8]

6. Francis Peck, *Desiderata Curiosa* (London, 1779), p. 548.

7. Charles H. Cooper and Thompson Cooper, *Athenae Cantabrigienses* (Cambridge, England, 1858), 1:321; and Crabbe, *Some Materials for a History of the Parish of Thompson*, p. 94. The College of Arms, however, has no record of the granting of these arms, yet the fact that Pory bore arms is further attested to by an inscription in one of the books which he gave to the library at Oxford where he is described as "armiger." The Société Française D'Heraldique et de Sigillographie, Paris, reports that a Porrey family lived in Burgundy in 1696 and bore arms similar to those ascribed above. The family in France was believed to be of English origin.

8. J. H. R. Yardley, *Before the Mayflower* (London, 1931), p. 90; and Annie Lash Jester, *Adventurers of Purse and Person, Virginia, 1607–1625* (Princeton, N.J., 1956), p. 377. I have not delved extensively into the Pory genealogy, but a survey of wills in the Lincolnshire archives and in the Principal Probate Registry, London, re-

At the beginning of the Easter term in 1588, when he was sixteen years old, John Pory was admitted to Gonville and Caius College, Cambridge, in the rank of pensioner.[9] Since its founding in 1348 by Edmund de Gonville of Norfolk, a number of the benefactors of the college had been Norfolk men, and the master during Pory's residence was Thomas Legge of Norwich.[10] In 1592 young Pory received the degree of bachelor of arts, and in 1595 he was granted the master of arts degree.[11] On 18 April 1610, by reason of "the reputation of his learning, and his skill in the modern languages, not very usual among the scholars of that age," Pory, together with his more widely known contemporary, John Donne, was incorporated master of arts at a convocation at the University of Oxford.[12]

veals numerous traces of the family for many years. For generation after generation the names John, William, Robert, and Peter occur frequently, and so many of them were living at the same time that only careful work could untangle all the lines. The name today appears to be excessively rare if, indeed, it has not entirely disappeared. In 1807 one Francis Porie, a merchant, lived in Tarboro, North Carolina, but efforts to trace his origin have been unsuccessful. He was dead by 1810, and his son-in-law, Daniel Redmond, settled his estate. In 1956 a Mr. Poorie retired as organist at Cleethorpes, Lincolnshire, but his grandfather had gone to England from Italy in the early nineteenth century.

9. John Venn and John A. Venn, *The Book of Matriculations: A Catalogue of Those Who Have Been Matriculated or Been Admitted to Any Degree in the University of Cambridge from 1544 to 1649* (Cambridge, England, 1913), p. 538. A student who was admitted as a pensioner was one who paid his own way. Students were admitted in three ranks: (1) fellow commoners, those holding fellowships; (2) pensioners; and (3) sizars, those receiving an allowance in return for which they often performed menial services. "*Pensioners* ... are most commonly Gentlemen of *Quality* or at least large fortunes" (Edmund Carter, *The History of the University of Cambridge* [London, 1753], p. 5).

10. Joseph Wilson, *Memorabilia Cantabrigiae* (London, 1803), p. 63; Carter, *The History of the University of Cambridge*, pp. 123–25, 131.

11. Venn and Venn, *Alumni Cantabrigiensis*, 3:383.

12. Henry Maty, *A New Review with Literary Curiosities and Literary Intelligence* 5 (February 1784):124; Andrew Clark, ed., *Register of the University of Oxford* (Oxford, 1887), 2:358. Pory and Donne may have first become acquainted as students at Cambridge. They remained on friendly terms for many years, and Pory delivered a number of letters to Donne at various times and from him to other persons. Donne mentioned Pory a number of times in his own letters (John Donne, *Letters to Several Persons of Honour* [London, 1651], pp. 56, 126, 246, 262–63; R. C. Bald, *John Donne, A Life* [New York, 1970], pp. 47, 227, 247–48, 259n.). Donne's twenty-line poem, "To Mr. J. P.," may have been addressed to Pory, although certain allusions do not fit the known facts of Pory's life (*The Poetical Works of Dr. John Donne, Dean of St. Paul's London* [Edinburg, Scotland, 1779], 3:166). The families of the two may have had an acquaintance of long standing. In 1562 one Richard Porye of Wood Street, London, bequeathed "to John Done ii of the better partes of silver spoons" (Prerogative Court of Canterbury, 2 Chayre).

Rubbing courtesy of C. P. H. Wilson, Thetford

These initials, perhaps those of John Pory, were carved on one of the stalls against the north wall of the chancel in Thompson church. Norwich museum experts have assigned the approximate date of 1600 to them.

Mrs Margaret Pory, died 1598.

Gentleman's Magazine *(February, 1819)*

Drawing of the monumental brass of Mrs. Margaret Pory (1542 or 1544 to 1598) in Tottington Church, Norfolk. She was the wife of Luke Unger and probably was the Margaret Pory who was the sister of William, John Pory's father.

John Porie. 1557.

John Lamb, Master's History of Corpus Christi, *opp. p. 85.*

The Pory arms as ascribed to Dr. John Pory (1503–70) were described as "Sable guttée d'eau a saltire Or."

John Venn, Biographical History of Gonville and Caius College, *vol. 3.*

An early seventeenth-century view of Gonville and Caius College.

After receiving his second degree from Gonville and Caius in 1595, Pory became an instructor in Greek at the college.[13] The only surviving evidence of his teaching, however, is an entry in the bursar's book for the period which shows a payment made to him. With the exception of a brief marginal note in the section entitled "A Description of Places Undescribed by John Leo" in Pory's translation of *A Geographical Historie of Africa*, little further indication has been found of his knowledge of Greek. On the other hand there is extensive evidence that he was proficient in several other languages than Greek. The use of Latin throughout his various writings was not unusual for a man of his education at that time, yet in his later years his Latin was often a little irregular, sometimes having a Greek construction. The ease with which he used both French and Italian is often indicated, as, for example in his letter of 16 July 1613 to Sir Thomas Edmondes, and in another of 3 February 1617 from Sir Henry Wotton, who was then in Venice, to Sir Ralph Winwood. "Mr. Porie, secretary to the ambassador [Paul Pindar] at Constantinople," Wotton wrote, "took pains to translate the King's book against the Cardinal Peron [*Déclaration du ... Roy Jacques ... pour le droit des Rois et indépendance de leurs Couronnes, contra la harangue d'illustrisime Cardinal du Perron, &c.* (London, 1615)], out of French into Italian, upon request of the Venetian ambassador there, who had taken much pleasure at certain passages thereof, which had been told him."[14] A little more than a year later Thomas Busher, in a letter to Ambassador Sir Dudley Carleton at The Hague, expressed his regret at being unable to obtain for him "the French booke which Mr. Porye saith your lordship is desireous to have."[15] On 14 January 1620 Pory closed a letter to Sir Edwin Sandys with several sentences in French. He sometimes also used Spanish proverbs and on occasion used even an old Anglo-Saxon word or one in Hebrew.

In 1597, at which time his association with Gonville and Caius College probably terminated, Pory began a study of cosmography and foreign history under the Reverend Richard Hakluyt, rector of the parish of Wetheringsett, Suffolk.[16] In "The Epistle

13. John Venn, *Biographical History of Gonville and Caius College, 1349–1897* (Cambridge, England, 1897), s.v. "Porye, John."

14. Logan Persall Smith, ed., *The Life and Letters of Sir Henry Wotton* (Oxford, 1907), 2:111. For a concise review of the literary activities of D. Perron see C. H. Herford and Percy Simpson, eds., *Ben Jonson* (Oxford, 1925), 1:67–69.

15. Thomas Busher to Sir Dudley Carleton, 16 September 1618, Public Record Office, SP Domestic, Jas. I, 14/99/1.

16. Cosmography was a popular term at this time. It embraced, as Sir Francis Bacon said, natural history as well as civil history, and he even included "Mathema-

The rectory at Wetheringsett, Suffolk, was the home of the Reverend Richard Hakluyt while Pory studied with him from 1597–1600. The right-hand portion of the house dates from about 1500; the section on the left is a Victorian addition.

Dedicatorie" of *The Third and Last Volume of Voyages, Navigations, Traffiques, and Discoveries of the English Nation,* dated 1 September 1600, Hakluyt wrote, "Now because long since I did foresee, that my profession of divinities, the care of my family and other occasions might call and divert me from these kinde of endevours, I have for these 3. yeeres last past encouraged and furthered in these studies of Cosmographie and forren histories, my very honest, industrious and learned friend M. Iohn Pory, one of

---

tics, in respect of the comiates and configurations of the heavens, beneath which the regions of the World be." Peter Heylyn wrote that it consisted of history, geography, politics, theology, chronology, and heraldry—that it "was not unlike a large-scale *survey*" (F. Smith, *The Historical Revolution, English Historical Writing and Thought, 1580–1640* [New York, 1962], 161). In 1594 cosmography was defined as "the description . . . of heaven and earth, and all that is contained therein" (*The Oxford English Dictionary,* s.v. "Cosmography").

A GEOGRAPHICAL
HISTORIE of AFRICA,

Written in Arabicke and Italian
by Iohn Leo a More, borne
in Granada, and brought vp
in Barbarie.

Wherein he hath at large described, not onely the qualities, situations, and true
distances of the regions, cities, townes, mountaines, riuers, and other places
throughout all the north and principall partes of Africa; but also the
descents and families of their kings, the causes and euents of their warres,
with their manners, customes, religions, and ciuile gouernment, and
many other memorable matters : gathered partly out of his owne di-
ligent obseruations, and partly out of the ancient records and Chronicles
of the Arabians and Mores.

Before which, out of the best ancient and moderne writers, is prefixed a generall
description of Africa, and also a particular treatise of all the maine lands
and Isles vndescribed by Iohn Leo.

And after the same is annexed a relation of the great Princes, and the manifold religions
in that part of the world.

Translated and collected by Iohn Pory, lately
of Goneuill and Caius College
in Cambridge.

LONDINI,
Impensis Georg. Bishop.
1 6 0 0

Title page of Pory's major geographical work.

At Home and Abroad ∾ 11

special skill and extraordinary hope to perform great matters in the same, and beneficial for the common wealth."[17]

Publications

Hakluyt quite obviously had selected Pory to be his successor and had been training him to carry on the work of collecting and publishing travel accounts which Hakluyt had begun more than ten years earlier and which rapidly brought him great renown. Pory assisted Hakluyt in the preparation of his volume of *Voyages* which was published in London in 1600. Pory himself, moved to do so by Hakluyt, also worked on the translation of *A Geographical Historie of Africa Written in Arabicke and Italian by Iohn Leo A More* which was published about ten weeks after Hakluyt's volume. Both of these significant works came from the press of George Bishop, one of the best London printers of the time. In spite of such a promising beginning, however, Hakluyt's hopes for Pory were not realized. He produced only one other related work, *An Epitome of Ortelius*, and it remained for Samuel Purchas to carry on Hakluyt's work.

Pory's translation of the lengthy work on Africa, nevertheless, must be counted one of his major accomplishments; it was certainly something that gained for him an early reputation as a writer, geographer, and translator. Hakluyt appreciated the importance of Africa in the East Indian trade, and he understood how useful bases there might be to English merchants, particularly to those who formed the East India Company. This book on that little-known region was designed to serve a good purpose.[18]

John Leo, the author of the book which Pory translated, was also known as Leo Africanus. Born in Spain, he traveled widely in Turkey, Arabia, and North Africa. While returning from Egypt in 1518 he was captured by pirates who ultimately presented him as a slave to Pope Leo X. In Rome he was converted to Christianity, mastered both Latin and Italian, and soon came under the influence of Giovanni Ramusio, a scholar and traveler who published geographical works. Leo's manuscript description of Africa which he was carrying with him when captured was originally written in Arabic, but in Rome in 1526 he translated it into Italian. His work dealt with only those parts of Africa north of the equator that he

17. Richard Hakluyt, *The Third and Last Volume of Voyages, Navigations, Traffiques, and Discoveries of the English Nation* (London, 1600), A3.
18. John Parker, *Books to Build an Empire* (Amsterdam, 1965), p. 166.

had actually seen or about which he had heard what he felt to be reliable information from travelers. Ramusio included the Italian translation, *Descrizione dell'Affrica*, in the first volume of his own book of travel, *Delle Navigationi et Viaggi*, published in 1550. It was primarily Ramusio's edition of Leo which Pory used in making his English translation, although he also consulted the Latin version.

Before Pory's English translation appeared, Leo's work had already gained wide popularity in Europe. Books of travel and exploration were eagerly read, and a growing interest in material of this nature reached a peak only after the age of exploration came to a close. Six years after Ramusio published Leo it was translated into French, though with a different arrangement of the contents. Two editions of this translation, beautifully printed and bound, appeared at Antwerp in 1556; and before the end of the year, John Florio, rector of the Grammar School in Antwerp, prepared a Latin version. Other editions appeared within the next few years, but it remained for Pory to put it into English nearly half a century after it was first published.[19]

In 1896 the Hakluyt Society published Pory's translation of Leo in a three-volume edition under the editorship of Robert Brown, an English geographer. Brown pointed out several instances of poor translation which suggested that Pory had been misled not by the Italian printing of 1556, which he generally used, but by the Latin edition of Florio which had a number of unfortunate errors.[20] In 1613 Samuel Purchas reprinted much of Pory's translation in *Purchas His Pilgrimes*, but a marginal note informs the reader that "In divers places the translation is amended."[21]

In the typically ingratiating fashion of the day, Pory described his work as "the first fruits, or rather the tender budds and blossoms of my labours," and dedicated the book "to the Right Honorable sir Robert Cecil, Knight, principall Secretarie to her Majestie,

19. A bibliography of the translation of Leo's book into Italian, French, Latin, English, and German, as well as a list of other works by him and of monographs dealing with him is in Louis Massignon, *Le Maroc dans les Premières Années du XVIe Siècle, Tableau Geographique d'après Léon L'Africain* (Algiers, 1906), pp. 4–11.

20. Robert Brown, ed., *The History and Description of Africa . . . Done into English in the Year 1600, by John Pory* (London, 1896), 1:lix. In 1969 the Da Capo Press, Amsterdam and New York, published a facsimile reprint of the 1600 edition. The collation of the original 1600 edition is: [ ]⁴.a–e⁶, A–O⁶, Q–Z⁶, Aa–Nn⁶: one map.

21. Samuel Purchas, *Purchas His Pilgrimes. In Five Books. The Sixth Conuayning Navigations, Voyages, and Land-Discoveries, With other Historicall Relations of Africa. The Second Part* (London, 1625), p. 749.

Master of the Court of Wardes and Liveries, and one of her Highnes Most Honorable privie Counsell." Cecil was Hakluyt's patron as well as Pory's, and he had commended Hakluyt's work. Pory sought the secretary's protection of his "tender budds and blossomes ... least in this their winterly sprouting they might perhaps by some bitter blasts of censure be frost-nipped." The dedication was dated from London "this three and fortieth most joifull Coronation-day of her sacred Majestie. 1600."[22] This, of course, was a definite enough date for his contemporaries: 17 November, the anniversary of Elizabeth's accession, was long regarded as "the happiest day that ever England had."[23] Pory's book appeared at a very propitious time, when there was considerable interest in Africa. As he noted in the dedication, a nobleman from Morocco had called upon Queen Elizabeth earlier in the year, yet in 1601 the Queen ordered "negars and blackmoores" transported out of England.

By way of encouraging the acceptance of the work of his protété, Hakluyt supplied an "approbation" to Pory's translation:

> Being mooved to publish mine opinion as touching this present Historie of John Leo; I do hold and affirme it to be the verie best, the most particular, and methodicall, that ever was written, or at least that hath come to light, concerning the countries, peoples, and affairs of Africa. For which cause, and knowing well the sufficiencies of the translator, my selfe was the first and onely man that perswaded him to take it in hand. Wherein how diligently and faithfully he hath done his part, and how he hath enlarged and graded this Geographical historie out of others, the best Ancient, and moderne writers, by adding a description of all those African maine lands and isles, and other matters verie notable, which Iohn Leo himself hath omitted: I referre to the consideration of all judiciall and indifferent Readers.

22. The role of the patron in Elizabethan publication is discussed in H. S. Bennett, *English Books & Readers, 1558 to 1603* (Cambridge, England, 1965), pp. 30–56. There were numerous reasons for seeking a patron, and financial support was not always most important. In this case Pory, an unknown scholar, may have felt that his book would receive attention if dedicated to Cecil, younger son of the recently deceased Baron Burghley, Queen Elizabeth's chief minister. His book, however, was one of four dedicated to Cecil that year. An intermittent relationship between Pory and Cecil, who became the Earl of Salisbury in 1605, continued for several years. On 7 March 1610, William Trumbull wrote Salisbury, "I send copy of a letter from Monsieur de la Faille late Secretary to the B[aron] of Hob[oken] at [Herberts?] in England to one Pory who is said to be employed about your Lordship" (Historical Manuscripts Commission, *Report on the Manuscripts of the Marquess of Downshire* [London, 1936], 3:256).

23. John Chamberlain to Sir Dudley Carleton, 17 November 1620, Norman E. McClure, ed., *The Letters of John Chamberlain* (Philadelphia, Pa., 1939), 2:330.

This was the only time that Hakluyt ever wrote such a prefatory note.[24]

Pory, as Hakluyt indicated, realized that Leo's work did not cover the whole of Africa, and a portion of the lengthy subtitle of his English translation takes note of this: *Before which, out of the best ancient and moderne writers, is prefixed a generall description of Africa, and also a particular treatise of all the maine lands and Isles undescribed by John Leo.* He consulted such more recent writers as Francisco Alvarez, Damião de Goes, Jan Huygen van Linschoten, and Duarte Lopes; he also drew from a report by Matthew Dresserus, a professor in the University of Leipzig, from another made by an ambassador sent by Pope Paul IV (1555–59) to Ethiopia, and from Abraham Hartwell's translation of Philippo Pigafetta's work on the Congo. Other new material which Pory added came from a number of unidentified sources. Pory is said to have modeled these contributions of his own on Giovanni Botero's *Della Relatione Universali* which appeared in 1592.[25] To Leo's work then, Pory added his own account of the country bordering the Red Sea and of Abyssinia, Lower Ethiopia, Zanzibar, Congo, Guinea, and Sierra Leone, as well as Madagascar, Ascension Island, Cape Verde Islands, Madeira Island and others in the South Atlantic. At the conclusion of his translation of the *Historie of Africa* Pory added "A briefe relation concerning the dominions, revenues, forces, and manner of government of sundry the greatest princes either inhabiting within the bounds of Africa, or at least possessing some parts thereof, translated, for the most part, out of Italian." To round out the work Pory also prepared a four-part discussion of "the manifold Religions professed in Africa," and he especially stressed the role of Christians in various parts of the continent.

Of his own contributions to the work of Leo, Pory wrote:

> Now as concerning the additions before and after this Geographicall Historie; having had some spare-howers since it came first under the presse; I thought good (both for this Readers satisfaction, and that Iohn Leo might not apeere too solitarie upon the stage) to bestowe a part of them in collecting and digesting the same. The chiefe scope of this my enterprize is, to make a briefe and cursorie description of all those maine lands and isles of Africa, which mine author in his nine bookes hath omitted. For he in very deed leaveth untouched all those parts of the African continent which lie to the south of the fifteene kingdoms of Negroes, and to the east of Nilus.

24. John Pory, *A Geographical Historie of Africa* (London, 1600), p. 57. David B. Quinn, ed., *The Hakluyt Handbook* (London, 1974), 1:314.

25. E. G. R. Taylor, *Late Tudor and Early Stuart Geography, 1583–1650* (London, 1934), p. 32.

For the manifestation whereof, I have (as truely as I could conjecture) in the mappe adjoned to this booke, caused a list or border of small prickes to be engraven; which running westward from the mouth of Nilus to the streights of Gibraltar, and from thence southward to the coast of Guinie, and then eastward to the banke of Nilus, and so northward to the place where it began: doth with advantage include all places treated of by Leo, and excludeth the residue which by way of Preface we have described before the beginning of his African historie. Likewise at the latter end I have put downe certaine relations of the great Princes of Africa, and of the Christian, Jewish, Mahumetan, and Gentilish religions there professed.[26]

Hakluyt was an archivist, a collector of travel accounts, and an editor who made only limited efforts to digest the works of others and present them for his readers. His pupil, Pory, however, at least in this case, succeeded in doing much more than that. His book on Africa has been called "a complete and systematic treatise."[27] Robert Brown regarded Pory's work as "an excellent specimen of Elizabethan English, lucid, quaint, and plain-spoken to the verge of what in these more conventional times, might be regarded as a little unrefined." He believed also that Pory let his personal feelings get the better of him on several occasions, especially when he inserted offensive remarks on that "great deceiver Mohamet," or took it upon himself to strengthen the epithets used by Leo. Commenting upon Leo himself as an observer and a writer, Brown believed that he was one of the few geographical writers of his age still worth reading, not only for the purposes of the historian or even for entertainment—both of which he considered Leo to be good for—but also for actual facts regarding the conditions of the countries and the habits of the people he wrote about.[28] This proved to be a correct appraisal if the judgment of late twentieth-century writers on Africa may be accepted.

Pory's translation of Leo Africanus remained the standard source of information about Africa in English until early in the nineteenth century when contemporary European travelers began to publish their own accounts. Many of the attributes popularly ascribed to Negroes found their origin in Pory's work: venery, addiction to treason, treachery, murder, and theft, as well as the allegation that they "leade a beastly kind of life."[29] A striking

26. Brown, *The History and Description of Africa*, 1:9.
27. George Bruner Parks, *Richard Hakluyt and the English Voyages* (New York, 1961), p. 183.
28. Brown, *The History and Description of Africa*, 1:lxxviii, cxi.
29. Winthrop D. Jordan, *White Over Black, American Attitudes Toward the Negro, 1550–1812* (Chapel Hill, N.C., 1968), pp. 33–35.

parallel may be seen between Pory's introductory account of John Leo and a number of significant points in Shakespeare's description of Othello's past. It has also been shown that Shakespeare's information about Egypt and the Nile in *Antony and Cleopatra* and the distinction between various Moors and Negroes came from Pory's work. The account of crocodiles in Pory furnished the basic information used by Shakespeare as well as by his contemporary dramatist, John Webster, whose *White Devil* in 1612 contained a section which is very close to a plagiarism of Pory.[30] Another playwright, Ben Jonson, also cited Leo Africanus as the source of his information about Africa. Jonson's *Masque of Blackness*, composed for presentation at Whitehall on 6 January 1605, had masquers representing Ethiopians and frequent mention of the River Niger. Another contemporary writer, Sir Walter Raleigh, cited Leo as one of the authorities consulted in the preparation of his *History of the World*, first published in 1614.

It was through Pory's translation that African geography was studied by many later explorers of that continent. Thomas Shaw (1694–1751), a noted English traveler in Africa, was among those who turned to Leo, as did Henry and Frederick Beechy, explorers of the Nile River between 1821 and 1823. By the late nineteenth century, however, more recent accounts were available, and, as Robert Brown noted in his introductory comments to Pory's work, Leo was regarded "merely as an historian—a personal witness of towns, and events, and manners which have passed away, or of circumstances which for four centuries have remained unaltered."[31] With the interest in black history in the twentieth century, Pory's work has enjoyed a renewed appreciation. Winthrop D. Jordan made use of some of his observations that reflected seventeenth-century attitudes toward blacks. Alvin M. Josephy, Jr., editor of *The Horizon History of Africa*, published in 1971, selected for inclusion numerous comments from Pory on the knowledge of Africa reflected by an Englishman in 1600.

An examination of Pory's own additions as well as his translation of Leo's work, with attention paid to unusual words and

30. Eldred Jones, *Othello's Countrymen, The African in English Renaissance Drama* (London, 1965), pp. 21–25. It was Lois Whitney, in "Did Shakespeare Know *Leo Africanus*?" *Publications of the Modern Language Association of America*, 37 (September, 1922):470–83, who first pointed out Shakespeare's use of Pory. This was further explored by Eldred Jones in *Othello's Countrymen* as well as in his *Elizabethan Image of Africa* (Charlottesville, Va., 1971).

31. Robin Hallet, *Africa to 1875* (Ann Arbor, Mich., 1970), p. 417; and Brown *The History and Description of Africa*, 1:lxxviii.

a comparison of these with the historical citations in the *Oxford English Dictionary*, suggest a number of interesting possibilities. In his book Pory used several words for which the *Oxford English Dictionary* records the earliest known use in 1599 and 1600 by Richard Hakluyt. Among these are *Cafri, Cafres*, or *Cafates* ("Kaffir"), *carovans* ("caravans"), *cinadre* ("cinnabar"), *cotton-wooll*, *ingenios* ("sugar-houses"), and *seraglios* ("palaces of Turks"), together with such old but long unused words as *bastinado* and *cotton*. The obvious conclusion is that Pory learned these words while he was studying under Hakluyt. Pory's use of other words not frequently encountered is cited by the *Oxford English Dictionary* as having been most recently used by such authors as Joannes Boemus, Richard Eden, John Frampton, John Gerard, and William Turner; their books may have been recommended to Pory by Hakluyt and from them he perhaps learned such words as *batata* ("potato"), *bitumen, hogge-fish, ichthypophagi, magazine* or *store-house, red sanders* ("red sandalwood"), and *sheque* ("sheik").

Pory also used a number of old words which were well on the way to becoming obsolete. The word *sithens*, meaning "since," was first noted in 1250, but it had apparently not been used for fifty years when Pory wrote, "Now sithens we are so far proceeded, let us take also a cursory and brief surveie [survey] of the lower or extreme Ethiopia." The editors of the *Dictionary* found *sithens* last used the next year after Pory's book appeared. His use of the word *stadios* ("stade"), an ancient measure of length, was an almost identical case. Pory wrote of the *Baduini* and the *Baduin-Arabians* as the inhabitants of inland Africa. The Bedouin of modern times had been known to the English during the Crusades, but they were apparently forgotten thereafter. The word was last used about 1400 until Pory resurrected it in 1600—a fact of which the editors of the *Dictionary* were unaware as their first citation after 1400 is dated 1603.

Several other words appear to have been used by Pory at an earlier date than the examples known to the editors. Where Pory learned these words, of course, is unknown, but his use of them in 1600 antedates the examples cited. Among such words are *aqua fortis, Angola, Cabala, cursory, hackney-iades* ("hackneyed" in the sense of hired or kept for hire), and *Sahara*.

The *Dictionary* ascribes to Pory the earliest known use of the words *henna, hippopotamus, promuscis* (the elephant's trunk), *sea-horses* (meaning "hippopotamus"), *stone-horse* ("stallion"), and *zebra.* Although he did not first use them, Pory's use of *gugelle* ("gazelle"), *jujubas, paps,* and *snowte* ("snout") is also cited.

If the discoveries of the editors of the *Dictionary* may be relied upon, Pory also employed many other words which had not been used for long periods of time. Among them are *Arrians* ("Aryans"), *bassa* ("bashaw" or "pasha"), *buffles* (apparently an early form of "buffalo"), *coromorants* or *sea-crowes, damsin-trees, dates* (the fruit), *dropsie, eben-wood* ("ebony"), *fitches* ("vetch"), *frankincense, galeots* ("galliots"), "*lee* ["lye"] made of ashes for soap" (*lee* in this sense was last reported used in 1426), *naughtie* ("bad or inferior material"), *Negroes* (which had been used earlier only in 1555 and 1580), *pelicans, taffeta,* and *Troglodytae.*[32]

Pory presented a copy of the *Geographical Historie of Africa* to the library of Gonville and Caius College with a printed paper inserted testifying to his regard for the college. The single-page presentation inscription in Latin, which is still in the book in the college library, credits his "fathers and brothers" there for any "genius, judgment, [or] erudition" which might be discovered in his work. These "lucubrations," he remarked in terms reminiscent of his rural background, were "the harvest, whatever it is worth, of your sowing and agriculture, and place it (if you will) in the granary of your library and after one (if God shall grant it) or two years, you will enjoy a much richer, and even a more mature gleaning."[33] The closing sentiments expressed here suggest that Pory was already at work on another book.

Some time before Queen Elizabeth's death on 24 March 1603, John Norton, a London printer who issued some of the most important books of the early seventeenth century, printed a small book of maps slightly larger than five by seven inches. Entitled *An Epitome of Ortelius His Theatre of the World, Wherein the principal regions of the earth are described in smalle Mappes,* it was issued anonymously and without a date. It has, however, on good evidence, been attributed to Pory.

A date prior to March 1603 must certainly be assigned as the latest possible date for its publication. The Library of Congress and others accept the date 1602.[34] The *Epitome of Ortelius* was dedi-

32. Examples of earliest usage cited in the *Oxford English Dictionary,* of course, represent only those known to the editors at the time of completion. Since the first volume appeared in 1884 countless examples of earlier usage have been discovered. See "Revising OED" in the *Times Literary Supplement,* 13 October 1972.

33. For the complete text of this presentation inscription see the microfiche letters.

34. Philip L. Phillips, *A List of Geographical Atlases in the Library of Congress* (Washington, 1909), 1:165. This date is also assigned in Taylor, *Late Tudor and Early Stuart Geography,* p. 219.

Reuerendo COLLEGII CAIO-
GONEVILLENSIS Cuſtodi,
ornatiſſimiſque ſocijs,plurimùm
ſibi obſeruandis.

N vobis quoque(PATRES &
FRATRES *) primitias haſce
meas, exiles illas quidem, vtpote
ſterili è ſolo, & lingua vernacula (quod
paſſim nunc moris eſt) editas , eq́ alienis
operibus verſas vtplurimùm & concinna-
tas.Si quid tamen ſit in illis,ſiue vertendis
ſiue colligendis, ingenij,iudicij , eruditio-
nis, totum illud quantulumcunque ſit, ve-
ſtrum(quorum alumnus tam nupèr fui)to-
tum,inquam,veſtrum eſt.*

*Accipite igitur lucubratiunculas iſtas,
prouentum qualemcunquè ſationis veſtræ
& agriculturæ, inque horreo (ſi placet)
reponite bibliothecæ veſtræ: & poſt annum (ſi* DEVS *dederit)vnum aut alte-
rum , multò vberiori, fortaſſe etiam ma-
turo magis fruemini ſpicilegio.*

Veſtri omnium obſeruantiſſimus

IOH. PORY.

Printed broadside that is laid in the copy of Pory's Historie of
Africa *that he presented to his old college, Gonville and Caius at
Cambridge.*

AN
EPITOME OF ORTELIVS
HIS THEATRE OF THE VVORLD, VVHEREIN
the principal regions of the earth are deſcribed in ſmalle Mappes.

VVith a brief declaration annexed to ech Mappe. And donne in more exaƈt manner, then the
lyke declarations in Latin, French, or other languages.

It is alſo amplyfied with new Mappes wanting in the Latin editions.

AT LONDON,
PRINTED BY IOHN NOR?????

Title page of Pory's second geographical work, probably published in 1602.

cated "To the Nobly-Descended, and Vertuously-Accomplished Mr. Richard Gargrave." Gargrave was knighted on 17 April 1603 by King James and of course would afterwards have been addressed as Sir Richard. A native of Yorkshire, Gargrave had served in Parliament from 1597 to 1598 and would serve again from 1604 to 1611, when Pory was also a member.

The copy of this book in the New York Public Library, bound in contemporary white vellum, has the crest of Queen Elizabeth stamped in gold on the cover, indicating that this was a special copy bound for her. The most important evidence that it was Pory who prepared this *Epitome of Ortelius*, however, is the fact that Queen Elizabeth's copy has "I: Pory." added in manuscript, apparently contemporary with the book, at the end of the dedication to Gargrave.

An entry in the register of the Company of Stationers of

TO THE NOBLY-DESCENDED, AND

VERTҰOVSLY-ACCOMPLISHED Mʳ. RICHARD GARGRAVE,

O S T vveorthy ſir, no ſooner did this ſtranger my friend ſet foot on Engliſh ſhore, but being deſirous to trauail North, I could not deuiſe vvhere he ſhould finde more condigne & reſpectiue intertainment then vnder your moſt fauourable roof. It appears by his many languages, namely Latin, Italian, French, Spaniſh, high & lovv Dutch, and novv laſtly Engliſh, that he hath ſometimes bin a traueler. And ſo indeed if you examin him throughly, you ſhall finde he hath, aſvvell by ſea as by land. In his diſcourſes he is vnlike the greateſt part of our trauellers, vvho vvith their tedious & fabulous narrations vvill bring either deafnes to your eares or ſlumber to your eyes. But this man ſpeakes nothing but matter, and that ſo ſuccinctly, as by his conference you may reap delight, & yet not hinder your affaires of importance or recreation. Giue him incouragement in the North, and ere long you ſhall ſee him come ouer in another habit, to try vvhat acceptance the ſouth vvill affourd him. Thus doing, you ſhall not onely grace him & benefit your country, but in all dutifull ſeruices you ſhall make mee his poore vvel-vviller,

Yours

Moſt truly deuoted.

I: Pory

Dedication page of Pory's Epitome of Ortelius *from the copy that was specially bound for Queen Elizabeth.*

London, 16 April 1602, shows that James Shawe, an unimportant London printer, "Entred for his copye under the hands of master Doctor Mountford and master Seton warden. A booke called *Epitome* Abrahami Ortelius to be translated into English." This book, "Now latly renewed and augmented by M. Coignet" and published in 1603, is not to be confused with Norton's. It was one of only seven books which Shawe published.[35]

Perhaps somehow related to the question of Pory's role in translating and preparing this small, thin *Epitome of Ortelius* is an entry in John Donne's humorous and satirical catalogue of imaginary works by his contemporaries. This catalogue, compiled sometime after 1603, contains this entry, "*Believe in thy havings, and thou hast them. A test for antiquities,* being a great book on very

35. Edward Arber, *A Transcript of the Register of the Company of Stationers of London, 1554–1640* (London, 1875–1894), 3:203; and Paul G. Morrison, *Index of Printers, Publishers and Booksellers in . . . A Short-title Catalogue* (Charlottesville, Va., 1950), p. 65.

small things, dictated by Walter Cope, copied out by his wife, and given a Latin dress by his amanuensis John Pory."[36] Both Pory and Gargrave at a later time are known to have been acquainted with Sir Walter Cope and his wife, but what Donne knew that prompted this comment is not revealed.

Another copy of *An Epitome of Ortelius* in the New York Public Library bears manuscript notes in faded ink on maps of Turkey and the Azores, both of which places Pory later visited. The possibility exists that he later discovered some error or some new information and jotted notes in the margin of this copy.

In 1598 Pory's future friends, John Chamberlain and Dudley Carleton, had been interested in the geographical works of Ortelius. "Ortelius his Thesaurus Geographicus is too bigg to be sent by an ordinarie messenger," Chamberlain wrote, "and therfore it must stay till your boat come or that you send other order."[37] Ortelius, who died in 1598 while Pory was with Hakluyt, had many English acquaintances. He was a good friend of Richard Hakluyt as well as of William Camden, with whom Pory was also acquainted.[38]

Another factor to be considered in ascribing the authorship of the *Epitome of Ortelius* to Pory is his own remarks on the geographical works of Ortelius. In commenting on previous historians and geographers who had found Leo's *Geographical Historie of Africa* useful, Pory wrote, "Were renowned Ortelius alive, I would under correction report me to him; whether his map of Barbarie and Biledulgeria, as also in his last Additament that of the kingdomes of Maroco and Fez, were not particularly and from point to point framed out of this present relation, which he also in two places at the least preferreth farre before all other histories written of Africa."[39] This suggests that Pory was so thoroughly familiar with the works of both Ortelius and Leo that he recognized facts which Ortelius had drawn out of Leo's work.

Pory listed the books that he had consulted in preparing the sections he added to Leo's history in order to round out the coverage on Africa. "I have helped my selfe out of sundrie discourses in ... Ortelius,"[40] he said, clearly indicating that he was using the works of Ortelius prior to 1600. English editions of Ortelius's

36. John Donne, *The Courtier's Library, or Catalogus Aribicorum incomparabilium et non vendibilium* (London, 1930), pp. 45–46.
37. Chamberlain to Carleton, 8 November 1598, in McClure, *Letters of John Chamberlain*, 1:52.
38. E. G. R. Taylor, *Tudor Geography, 1485–1583* (London, 1930), p. 88.
39. Brown, *The History and Description of Africa*, 1:8.
40. Ibid., 1:11.

Theatrum were available only after 1602 when the *Epitome* was published.

Brief epitomes of great books and English translations of important foreign works were very popular with the "unlearned reading public" in England—that is, those who could not read Latin—during the sixteenth and seventeenth centuries.[41] Pory was aware of this, and in his work with Leo Africanus and with Ortelius he helped supply these people with the means of satisfying their new thirst for knowledge.

Yet Pory's interest was not solely in past geographical explorations or histories of ancient lands. The eyes of Englishmen were turned westward to the New World where a colony landed on 13 May 1607. The whole of England must have waited eagerly for word from this small group deposited in the wilderness of Virginia. Captain Christopher Newport, who safely piloted the colony to its destination, sailed from Virginia on Monday, 22 June, returning to England.[42] Among the letters which he took back describing the new country was one addressed to John Pory from "a Duchman" who had gone over with the English. "Master Porie tells me," wrote Dudley Carleton, a member of Parliament, on 18 August 1607, "of a name given by a Duchman who wrote to him in Latin from the new towne in Verginia, Jacobopolis, and Master Warner hath a letter from Master George Percie who names theyr towne James-fort, which we like best of all the rest because it comes neere to Chemes-ford."[43]

The second charter granted the Virginia Company on 23 May 1609, lists "John Porie, gentleman" as one of the many grantees of the corporation which was known officially as "The Treasurer and Company of Adventurers and Planters of the City of London for the first Colony in Virginia."[44] Peter Pory, gentleman, perhaps Pory's uncle of that name, was one of the early settlers in Virginia, and one Robert Pory, perhaps another uncle, "adventured" £25 in the Virginia Company in 1618 or 1619.[45] Other events

41. Fussner, *The Historical Revolution*, p. 58.

42. Richard L. Morton, *Colonial Virginia* (Chapel Hill, N.C., 1960), 1:9–12.

43. Philip L. Barbour, ed., *The Jamestown Voyages Under the First Charter, 1606–1609* (Cambridge, England, 1969), 1:113–14. Pory was also a member of Parliament at this time.

44. Mattie Erma Edwards Parker, ed., *North Carolina Charters and Constitutions, 1578–1698* (Raleigh, N.C., 1963), p. 34.

45. Barbour, *Jamestown Voyages*, 2:397; and Susan M. Kingsbury, ed., *The Records of the Virginia Company of London* (Washington, 1906–35), 3:87, 332. The christening dates of both Peter and Robert Pory are recorded in the Thompson parish register.

intervened, however, and more than ten years passed before John Pory took any active part in the affairs of Virginia.

Member of Parliament

On 11 January 1604, King James issued a proclamation for the election of a parliament. Among other qualities which he desired in its members, he wanted them to be competent to act in all matters in the national interest and farsighted in the matter of religion. He demanded an honest election and wanted no outlaws or bankrupt men chosen. Sheriffs were directed to hold elections only in those boroughs with a population large enough to make a choice—apparently an attempt to combat some of the evils of the "rotten borough" system which had developed. And finally, after the election, all returns were to be delivered to the Court of Chancery—the next highest court to Parliament itself—where elections which had been run contrary to the proclamation were to be voided.[46]

The people of the ancient borough of Bridgwater in Somerset, a flourishing village even before the days of William the Conqueror, returned John Pory on 5 November 1605 to be their representative in the House of Commons in the place of their former member, Robert Bucking, who had recently died.[47] Another member from Somerset, Sir Edward Phelips, was Speaker of the House of Commons for this Parliament that James summoned to meet on 19 March 1604 and dissolved on 9 February 1611. Pory held his seat as a member of the House of Commons from the date of the return of his name until the dissolution.

Pory's comments on the activities of the Commons at this time are interesting in view of the fact that it was an extremely important session in the history of Parliament. His experience there stood him in good stead in 1619 when he was chosen Speaker of the first representative assembly ever to be convened in America.

An air of rebellion pervaded the whole of James's first parliament. In 1604 the House of Commons declared, "Our privileges and liberties are our right and due inheritance, no less than our very land and goods. . . . They cannot be withheld from us . . . but with apparent wrong to the whole state of the realm." Six years later the

46. Willard M. Wallace, *Sir Edwin Sandys and the First Parliament of James I* (Philadelphia, Pa., 1940), p. 20.
47. House of Commons, *Members of Parliament, Part I, Parliaments of England, 1213–1702* (London, [1888?]), p. 445.

members asserted that it was an "ancient general and undoubted right of Parliament to debate fully all matters which do properly concern the subject." In an attempt to curb the Crown's broadening powers, Commons asserted that the problem was "one of law simply" and had nothing to do with any "divinely conferred authority," thus initiating the long struggle between the Crown and the House of Commons.[48]

Pory's letter of 17 July 1610 to Sir Ralph Winwood, English agent to the States-General of Holland and later an outspoken leader of the House of Commons, gives a detailed account of the actions of the House at that time. The questions being discussed were considered to be very significant, and Pory felt that "this Day in the Success may prove either the happiest or unhappiest Parliament Day since his Majestye's coming in."

Six "Demandes" had been presented to the king for his approval before the Commons would enter "into the Bargaine" which James was trying to strike with them. "To the first and second (which were, that in case of Outlawrys and Attainders the Debts of the Delinquet should be first payd)" Pory wrote, "his Majesty was well pleased to grant them."

The next two demands made upon the king—that his servants might be arrested without royal authority and that no man be forced to lend money to the king or to give a reason why he would not—met with considerable royal resistance. James did not like their "Precedents of Antiquity to strengthen these Demands," and he was opposed to those "drawn from the Times of usurping or decaying Princes, or of People too bold and wanton." It would not be a good "Commonwealth," James told a delegation of members which called upon him, "where Subjects should be assured of all things and hope for nothing." He conceded, however, "that in Matters of Loans he would refuse no reasonable Excuse, nor should

48. Theodore K. Rabb, "Sir Edwin Sandys and the Parliament of 1604," *American Historical Review* 69 (April 1964):646–70; John W. Allen, *English Political Thought, 1603–1660* (London, 1938), 1:8, 26; Samuel R. Gardiner, ed., "Parliamentary Debates in 1610," *Camden Society Publications, Number 81* (Westminster, 1862), p. v; Williams M. Mitchell, *The Rise of the Revolutionary Party in the English House of Commons, 1603–1629* (New York, 1957), pp. 1–54. The best account of all of the work of James's first parliament is Wallace Notestein, *The House of Commons, 1604–1610* (New Haven, Conn., 1971). The copy of *A Record of some worthy proceedings: In the Honourable, Wise, and Faithfull Howse of Commons in the Late Parliament* ([Amsterdam?], 1611) in the Yale University Library contains an interesting typed note laid in which begins, "In this small tract of 48 pp. we have the record of the dissolution of the first Stuart Parliament, marking an epoch in our Constitutional History, and the final disappearance of the Tudor constitutional system."

King James I

my Lord Chamberlaine deny the arresting of any of his Majesty's Servants if just Cause were shewed."

The fifth condition presented to the king met his flat rejection. It was demanded that in criminal cases accused persons be given the right of presenting witnesses to clear themselves. James said that men would commit perjury for an ox or a sheep and certainly would do the same to save the life of a friend. He considered this to be "a Matter of Conscience" and he "could not part with it for mony." As matters developed this was a royal right which both he and Charles I exercised many times.

The final demand was granted by James with good grace. This concerned the repeal of an act of the reign of Henry VIII giving the king power to make "arbitrary lawes over the Welchmen." Since "their loyalty, faith & obedience was well knowen," Pory wrote Winwood, the king "would not leave a marke of Separation upon them in point of freedome."

Having thus gained most of what they demanded of the king, Parliament turned to what he desired of them. This they referred to as "the Price." He was seeking a set income so that he "would no more rise and fall like a marchant." In connection with the royal demands, the lord treasurer (Pory's old patron, Robert Cecil, now the Earl of Salisbury) read a short letter from the king, some "fragments" of which Pory remembered well enough to quote to Winwood.

The lord treasurer acted as spokesman for the king in this matter. He pointed out that the amount requested was £20,000 lower than a previous request, and since James had just granted Parliament "sundry demands of importance never dreamt on . . . it would beseem us to meet with our soveraigne halfe way." In conclusion the treasurer expressed his regard for the Commons and begged "excuse & pardon of you gentlemen . . . if any of you have conceived any mistaking to proceed out of these lips." Thereupon the House members began to depart without taking action on the royal request. The treasurer called the members back to say that he had just delivered the king's "final & peremptory resolution." He pointed out that "the Distance was little & bargain advantagious." If the House took no action the king "would instantly dissolve the parliament & would never make the like offer to this assembly." "So we all returned to the house," Pory reported, and "instantly putt it to the question, and yielded to give his Majesty a perpetual revenue of £200000 a yeare upon [certain] Conditions," and he listed eight concessions demanded by the Commons. These dealt

The House of Commons about 1610 when Pory was a member.

with such subjects as the Court of Wards, purveyance, informers, debts, claims to land, and the entering of pleas against the Crown. In conclusion, the subject having just been raised, Pory said, "Now remaines there to be resolved on the assurance, & with what cordes we shall binde Sampsons handes."

Pory's letter suggests that the House of Commons was heeding the wish expressed on 11 June 1610 by Sir Francis Bacon, a spokesman for the Crown, that "we might alter our corse, having now spent almoste 5 months in matters impertinent, and extravagant discourses, whearof some square, some long, some short, but all circular, for wee are there almost where wee first begunne."[49] Progress was being made by the House of Commons in the struggle

49. Gardiner, "Parliamentary Debates," p. 53.

against the king. Members worked out a system of committees to consider and report on bills before final action was taken.[50] Pory employed such a system when he was Speaker of the assembly in Jamestown in the summer of 1619.

Pory served in the second through fifth sessions of King James's first parliament: 5 November 1605 to 26 May 1606; 18 November 1606 to 4 July 1607; 9 February 1610 to 23 July 1610; and 16 October 1610 to 9 February 1611. During this period he served on five committees. Entries in the sparse journals of the House of Commons suggest that he served on more committees than most other members who were neither knight nor nobleman, but none of his assignments seems to have been of great significance. Perhaps the most benefit Pory received from membership on these committees, aside from the simple fact of learning how they operated, was the opportunity to become intimately acquainted with a number of prominent men. He served with Sir Edwin Sandys and Sir Thomas Smyth, both officials of the Virginia Company on one or more occasions. One of the matters referred to a committee on which both these men and Pory served was concerned with the transportation of commodities, a subject which may well have related to Virginia. Other members of this parliament with whom Pory was already acquainted or with whom he had later contact included Sir Walter Cope, Sir Robert Cotton, Sir Henry Montagu, Dudley Carleton, and Sir Richard Gargrave.[51] The list of grantees of the charter of the Virginia Company of London, 23 May 1609, reads almost like a membership roll of the House of Commons at this time, and without doubt Pory was well acquainted with many of them.

While he was a member of Parliament, Pory frequently enjoyed the social life of London. His accounts of two noteworthy events during his first year in the city illustrate the lavishness of royal entertainment as well as his ability to observe and describe events. A series of entertainments during the first week of January 1606 celebrated the marriage of Robert Devereux, Earl of Essex, fourteen-year-old son of the late Earl who was a favorite of Queen Elizabeth, to Frances Howard, thirteen-year-old daughter of Thomas

50. Wallace, *Sir Edwin Sandys*, pp. 27–28. For contemporary accounts of the 1610 session of Parliament see Elizabeth Read Foster, *Proceedings in Parliament, 1610* (New Haven, Conn., 1966).

51. *Journals of the House of Commons. From November the 8th 1547 . . . to March the 2nd 1628. . . .* (n.p., n.d.), 1:291, 301, 315–16, 330, 333, 379, 381, 412, 439.

Howard, Earl of Suffolk.[52] Ben Jonson wrote a masque, *Hymenaei, or the Solemnities of Masque and Barrier at a Marriage* for the occasion. Stage settings and costumes were designed by the noted architect and designer Inigo Jones, and, as Pory observed, his machinery for lowering some of the masquers to the stage was greatly admired. Music was under the direction of Alphonso Ferrabosco, a popular musician of the day, and the dances were supervised by Thomas Giles. Shakespeare knew this masque and employed one resembling it in *The Tempest*.[53] The union celebrated by Jonson in *Hymenaei* was more than just the union of two important families in England. It was designed to symbolize "the new union of England and Scotland, the union of King James and his kingdom, the cosmic union wrought by the power of love."[54]

The night after the masque was presented guests were entertained at a mock barrier in which men pretended to fight with short swords. The Duke of Lennox led the men fighting for Truth while the Earl of Sussex led those for Opinion. Members of both teams were dressed in blue, wore white socks, were crowned with palm wreaths, and carried a palm bough in their hands.[55]

The masque was presented on Twelfth Night, 5 January 1606, and Pory's letter to Sir Robert Cotton two days later described both events in considerable detail. He continued to follow court gossip and soon reported a split in the team of Ben Jonson-Inigo Jones. Jones, standing higher in favor at court, discarded Jonson as the author of his court masques and other entertainments because, according to Pory, Jones was "angry with him for putting his own name before his in the title-page." Jonson, in a fit of revenge, then made Jones the subject of several bitter satires.[56]

On Thursday, 17 July 1606, Christian IV, king of Denmark, arrived in England on a visit to his sister, Queen Anne, wife of King

52. This marriage was annulled in 1613, followed by a shameful second marriage of the bride, murder, and a great public scandal which did not leave even the royal family untainted (Enid Welsford, *The Court Masque* [Cambridge, 1927], p. 178; and Lawrence Stone, *The Crisis of the Aristocracy, 1558–1641* [Oxford, 1965], pp. 651, 655, 667–68).

53. William Gifford, ed., *The Works of Ben Jonson* (London, 1875), 7:73–74; William A. Armstrong, "Ben Jonson and Jacobean Stagecraft," in *Jacobean Theatre* (New York, 1960), p. 48–49; and Welsford, *The Court Masque*, pp. 335–36. The complete masque, with explanatory notes, also appears in Stephen Orgel, ed., *Ben Jonson: The Complete Masques* (New Haven, Conn., 1969), pp. 75–106, 514, 523; as well as in Stephen Orgel and Roy Strong, *Inigo Jones, The Theatre of the Stuart Court* (Berkeley, Calif., 1973), 1:105–13.

54. *A Book of Masques* (Cambridge, England, 1967), pp. 2–3.

55. Text and directions for both the masque and the barrier may be found in Gifford, *Works of Ben Jonson*, 7:45–78.

56. Welsford, *The Court Masque*, p. 220.

James. A week later Robert Cecil, now newly created Earl of Salisbury, began a four-day period of feasting and entertainment for the royal family and their guest at Theobalds, his home in Hertfordshire. When the royal party arrived, they were greeted at the gates of the estate with a song of welcome sung under an artificial oak of silk. Just what part Pory took in this lengthy entertainment is not made clear. The detailed description of one of the excursions in his letter of 12 August to Sir Robert Cotton, however, suggests that he was present.

Travel and Employment Abroad

Before Parliament was prorogued on 4 July 1607, Spanish emissaries were in London discussing a treaty of peace, but England also wanted the Dutch to be consulted. Commissioners were designated to go to the United Provinces to discuss the proposed treaty and to invite their participation. Four members of the late parliamentary session—Sir Hugh Beeston, Sir Walter Cope, Dudley Carleton, and John Pory—decided to accompany the commissioners. Carleton anticipated that his presence on such a mission, even in an unofficial capacity, might result in some form of employment in the immediate future. Beeston withdrew before plans had progressed very far; so the Privy Council issued a passport to Cope, Carleton, and Pory. Carleton reported everything in readiness for the journey; Lady Cope had packed "jumbles and biscuit-bread ready baked," and both she and her daughter, Betty, had reconciled themselves to being left alone for a time and dried their tears. For the trip Pory purchased new luggage "besides jerkin, hose, cloak, hood, and bases all of a piece." He bought two new tablets as well and also packed his old ones with his notes from the late sitting of Parliament still in them. He took "solemn leave" of Prince Henry, assorted lords and ladies, and "all the ambassadors" and collected large packets of letters to be delivered in the Low Countries and in France. The trio met at the appointed place in the Strand to begin the ride to the coast, intending to cross the channel to Calais. At the last moment, while waiting to saddle up, a letter stopping them arrived from the secretary of state, Sir Robert Cecil (Lord Salisbury). Carleton commented that Salisbury mentioned "many important considerations" which prompted this action. Among them: "hasty posting to and fro being now so straitened in time, a winter passage by sea at our return, and danger of losing more by absence than were like to be gained by this short experience." To soften what must have been a great disappointment, Salisbury invited the three men to come "in all haste" to join him and other friends of theirs "to make an end ... of a merry progress." The treaty in which Pory and his friends were interested was signed in due course that year, and it contained provisions which were to be of benefit to Pory and Carleton in the near future. Under its terms Catholic countries were opened to English travelers, and after many years of uncertainty it now became possible for Englishmen to travel on the Continent with every expectation of doing so in safety.[57]

Having missed this opportunity for foreign travel with his friends, Pory perhaps contented himself with the pleasures of London between sessions of Parliament. Ten months of 1610–11 found him again in the Commons, and he was in Oxford briefly in 1610 for a convocation. King James ultimately dissolved his first parliament on 9 February 1611, and on 21 May "A lisense to travell for John Porye gentleman for 3 yeares with two servants and £30 in money" was granted. To leave the kingdom it was necessary to have the permission of the king, and this was obtained through a license to travel signed by one of the secretaries of state in ordinary cases, but by the king himself for noblemen and their families.[58]

In the brief time he had before leaving England, Pory attempted to interest his friend Sir Dudley Carleton in a manufacturing scheme which promised great wealth. The Reverend William Lee in 1598 had invented the first stocking frame, but Queen Elizabeth refused him a patent for fear of putting the country's countless handknitters out of work. She also was displeased with the coarse weave of the stockings and encouraged Lee to improve his machine.[59] Pory learned in 1611 as he was preparing to go abroad that Southcott Waymouth, an Englishman living in Venice, had invented an improved machine which would make a good quality silk stocking. Waymouth and some friends who had been associated with him in this venture were anxious to establish themselves in England or to secure financial backing to enable them to work in Venice. Carleton's brother, George, was approached by

57. Maurice Lee, Jr., ed., *Dudley Carleton to John Chamberlain, 1603–1624, Jacobean Letters* (New Brunswick, N.J., 1972), pp. 96–98; McClure, *Letters of John Chamberlain*, 1:245; John Walter Stoye, *English Travellers Abroad, 1604–1667* (London, 1952), p. 22.

58. Public Record Office. S.P. 38/10/1. Edward R. Turner, *The Privy Council of England in the Seventeenth and Eighteenth Centuries, 1603–1784* (Baltimore, Md., 1928), 1:151.

59. Milton and Anna Grass, *Stockings for a Queen, The Life of the Rev. William Lee, the Elizabethan Inventor* (London, 1967), pp. 59–78, 87–114.

Pory with this information, and in a letter of 4 July 1611 to Sir Dudley, George related the details. Sir Dudley in the previous October had become the English ambassador in Venice, and Pory hoped that he might want to take advantage of the opportunity to invest in this undertaking. Sir Michael Green, a merchant, urged haste in the decision as a messenger from home, the son of one Joyner of Cuddesdon near Oxford, had already been negotiating with Marc' Antonio Correr, who until May had been the Venetian ambassador in England but had now returned home. Sir Henry Saville, upon learning of the opportunity, even pressed him "to undertake the matter for you," George wrote. But he decided "we durst not playe the mrchant adventurers for you wthout letters of advise passing to & fro beforehand." Upon learning of George's action, Carleton's friends "complayned of the heavyness of the Inglish nature . . . in not beinge apt to apprehend good oportunytye & slow to adventure though such pregnant likelyhodes." Time for correspondence ran out, and Pory went abroad without pursuing this matter further.[60]

Ireland

Dorothy Lady Cope, writing to Sir Dudley Carleton from London on 24 June reported that "Porie is not in Towne but prepares him to sail for Irland to goe with my Lo Carew."[61] George Lord Carew at this time was master of the ordnance, and, on the same day that Lady Cope wrote, King James issued instructions sending him to Ireland to obtain information "for the better direction how to proceed in our Service." Among other things he was to determine what laws might be necessary for Ulster and which Irish laws should be abolished. The Ulster plantation was of particular concern to King James, and Lord Carew was expected to report on those actions which might bring the best results in its secure establishment. He was specifically instructed to seek forfeited land to which Ulster natives might be moved. Pory accompanied Carew and before the end of July was given the special assignment of delivering terms of pardon to Peter Easton, a pirate who had arrived

---

60. Public Record Office. S.P. 14/65/9. Waymouth in 1612 secured a patent in Venice to operate his knitting machine there for thirty years (Horatio F. Brown, ed., *Calendar of State Papers and Manuscripts, relating to English affairs, existing in the archives and collections of Venice* [London, 1905], 12:357–58).

61. Public Record Office. S.P. 14/64/54.

Pacata Hibernia *(Dublin, 1810), 2: frontispiece*

George Carew, master of the ordnance, whom Pory accompanied to Ireland in 1611.

at the southwestern tip of Ireland between Crookhaven and Schull with thirteen ships recently seized from London and Dover merchants. Pory was to "bring back their full resolution therein." After several weeks Carew seems to have grown apprehensive about Pory's welfare; on 16 August from Derry near the northern tip of Ireland, he wrote to Lord Salisbury that he wished Pory had returned.

On 30 June King James had approved the giving of protection to Easton in return for the surrender of the ships, and Pory, sailing in a merchant ship, delivered the official documents to the pirate. Pory rejoined Carew at the end of the first week in September. Easton seems to have accepted the terms, but before long he returned to his old ways. When Pory next encountered Captain Easton, they were in Turin in July 1613. Easton was then in the unlawful service of some of the cities of Italy.

Pory and Lord Carew had both become members of the Virginia Company under the charter of 1609, and they had served together in the recent parliament. They became lifelong friends and were "on such terms of intimacy" that Pory was able to "remonstrate freely against his permitting, as Master of the Ordnance, some of the field guns to be sent from the Tower to the Morisco chief of Sallee, previously a nest of pirates, for the redemption of English captives."[62]

France

On the very last day of 1611, John Chamberlain wrote that "Master Poorie is gone or going over into Fraunce and so into Italie about some pettie prieng employment." Late in January 1612 he was in Amiens where he visited John Donne,[63] but before the end of the month Chamberlain had more definite information to report. "If you have not heard it, Pories employment into Fraunce was to carrie a treatise of the bishop of Elies and Casabons to the Cardi-

62. J. S. Brewer and William Bullen, eds., *Calendar of the Carew Manuscripts Preserved in the Archepiscopal Library at Lambeth* (London, 1873), pp. 68, 69; C. W. Russell and John P. Prendergast, eds, *Calendar of State Papers, Relating to Ireland* (London, 1877), 4:75, 89, 95, 100; Thomas Birch, *The Court and Times of James I* (London, 1849), 1:243; Brown, *Calendar of State Papers ... Venice*, 12:xxi–xxii, 176, 218; *Memorials of Affairs of State in the Reigns of Q. Elizabeth and K. James I. Collected (chiefly) from the Original Papers of the Right Honourable Sir Ralph Winwood* (London, 1725), 3:286–87.

63. Chamberlain to Carleton, in McClure, *Letters of John Chamberlain*, 1:326; Donne, *Letters to Several Persons of Honour*, p. 126.

nall Perron in aunswer of a certain letter of his sent to the King, and withall goode part of Quene Elizabeths life, (collected with the help of Sir Robert Cotton and written by Clarenceaux),[64] for a present to Thaunus, to be inserted into his workes: which if it so prove Camden hath taken a deale of paine to small purpose, and is like to loose the honor and fruit of his labours, to see them drowned and swallowed up in such a gulfe."[65]

Jacques Davy, Cardinal du Perron of France, had been guilty of "disrespectful carriage" toward King James. In an attempt to censure him, as King James had "punished Wentworth for unseemly language against the late King of France,"[66] a "treatise," written by Lancelot Andrewes, Bishop of Ely, and Isaac Casaubon, one of the leading scholars of Europe and then resident of London, was prepared for delivery by Pory.[67]

For a new edition of his *Histoire de son Temps*, published first in parts in Latin beginning in 1604 with the title *Historia sui Temporis*, Pory also delivered to the French historian, Jacques-Auguste de Thou, "ten books of the MS commentaries, of the reign of Queen Elizabeth."[68] This study of Elizabeth's reign had been written by the historian William Camden, but it was sent to France in Pory's care by Casaubon. It was reported at the time that Sir Robert Cotton had also assisted in the preparation of the material on Queen Elizabeth, but it was soon revealed that Cotton had not completed his work in time for it to be sent over.[69] Pory wrote Cotton from Paris on 2 February 1612 concerning de Thou's comments on Cotton's contribution which must have just been received, and the same subject was discussed again in a letter of 30 June. The great work by de Thou went through a number of editions and printings in England for twenty years following its first appearance there in 1615.[70]

Pory remained in Paris for more than a year. On 11 August 1612 Chamberlain commented that it had been a long time since he

64. William Camden, noted English antiquary and historian, who held the position of Clarencieux, second King-of-Arms.

65. Chamberlain to Carleton, 29 January 1612, in McClure, *Letters of John Chamberlain*, 1:332.

66. Mary Anne Everett Green, ed., *Calendar of State Papers, Domestic Series, of the Reign of James I, 1611–1618* (London, 1858), p. 270.

67. This is perhaps no. 4740 or 4741 in A. W. Pollard and G. R. Redgrave, *A Short-title Catalogue of Books Printed in England, Scotland, and Ireland . . . 1475–1640* (London, 1950).

68. Maty, *A New Review*, 5 (February, 1784):125.

69. Samuel Kinser, *The Works of Jacques-Auguste de Thou* (The Hague, 1966), pp. 108–9.

70. Pollard and Redgrave, *Short-title Catalogue*, nos. 4496–502.

had heard of Pory, but at least understood that "he lies ligier at Paris" maintained by his old friend George, Lord Carew.[71] Pory was probably serving as an agent or correspondent for Lord Carew, either in a private business venture or to aid him in his position of master-general of the ordnance by observing developments in France.

It was while he was in Paris that Pory witnessed, and actually participated in a minor way, in a disputation between the Reverend Daniel Featly, Protestant, and Richard Smith, Roman Catholic. Both were English, Featly was chaplain to Sir Thomas Edmondes, the English ambassador, while Smith, who had recently arrived from Rome, soon settled at the College d'Arras to preside over a small group of English priests engaged in writing controversial works. The formal disputation, conducted under the same rules as those which prevailed at Oxford, took place in the chamber of one Knevet or Knyvet, "an honest & vertuous Gentleman the[n] living in that Cittie." Knevet had observed the Roman Catholic Church in Paris and commented "that before Luther all *knowne* Churches did beleeve that which he saw there in Fraunce openlie professed." With his half-brother, John Foord, Knevet arranged a meeting between Featly and Smith.

To the session at noon on 4 September 1612 Smith brought his cousin, one Rainer, afterwards a doctor of divinity. In addition to Knevet, Foord, Rainer, and Pory, the meeting was also attended by Thomas Rant (native of Norwich in Norfolk and a student at Caius College when Pory had been an instructor in Greek), Henry Constable, and Ben Jonson, the poet (who was then tutor on a foreign tour to Sir Walter Raleigh's son). Others, both English and French, attended, and young Raleigh probably was among them. (Featly, incidentally, had also been young Raleigh's tutor at Oxford.) Featly called the Reverend Pierre du Moulin, noted French Protestant, to be present, and he first agreed to do so but afterwards changed his mind.

Under the rules agreed upon, Featly was to dispute and Smith to defend. It was expected that at a second encounter the positions would be reversed, but this meeting never took place. Featly, a young man of thirty, had already gained notoriety for his brash attacks upon Roman Catholic doctrines. He supported the view "that the bodie & blood of our Saviour be not in the Eucharist truelie according to the veritie and substance of the thing signified

71. Chamberlain to Carleton, in McClure, *Letters of John Chamberlain*, 1:377–78. *Leiger* or *ledger* meant "a permanent resident."

by those names, but the Eucharist is a signe & figure of it onlie." Smith, sixteen years older, a doctor of divinity and professor of philosophy, maintained "that in the holy Eucharist, there is the bodie and blood of our blessed Saviour *trulie, reallie, and substantiallie*." It was Featley's purpose "to prove the Catholike *tenet* to be false." After a debate lasting from noon until about seven o'clock, during which ancient and modern writers were cited, the disputation ended. Both Protestant and Roman Catholic versions were published, and both speakers claimed to have prevailed. The account supporting Smith records that Featley was no match for the more experienced older man, and that Featley even "brought his arguments in a paper, & Master Porie for pittie helpt him out."[72]

Pory and Jonson appear to have kept careful notes on the course of the discussion, and in 1630, at a very significant time, they prepared them for publication. They produced a twenty-two-page account of what had occurred and published it when Dr. Richard Smith was very much in the public eye. In 1625 Smith became Vicar Apostolic for England with the title of Bishop of Chalcedon. He soon established a system of church government that included a group of administrative assistants to the bishop, vicars, archdeacons, notaries, and registrars. Headquarters were set up in Bedfordshire from which he made trips in many directions but seldom traveled to London. Smith was not acceptable to the Jesuits in England nor to many of the laity. The rising activity of Roman Catholics and the fact that Queen Henrietta Maria was of that faith gave rise to suspicions of a Papist plot. The publication at that critical time of the Pory-Jonson account of the disputation eighteen years earlier, in which Smith had attacked the Protestant faith, served to alert both Anglicans and dissenters as to the kind of man he was. With many of his own faith opposed to him and certainly in the face of opposition from the Establishment, Smith in the summer of 1631 departed for Paris where he spent the remainder of his life. England had been saved from the influence of a Roman Catholic bishop.[73]

Pory noted in the published account that Smith had not obeyed the rules of the disputation. Instead he had made "by-

72. In time Featley mastered the art of disputation, and he could also put his opponents in their place with his pen. James Howell, writing to Featley on 1 August 1644, remarked, concerning a pamphlet by Featley, "Never poor Cur was toss'd in a Blanket as you have toss'd that poor Coxcombe in the Sheet you pleas'd to send me" (James Howell, *Epistolae Ho-Elianae: Familiar Letters Domestick and Foreign* [London, 1737], p. 442).
73. Martin J. Havran, *The Catholics in Caroline England* (Stanford, Calif., 1962), pp. 55, 67, 76, 85–90.

THE
SVMME
AND
SVBSTANCE OF
A DISPVTATION BE-
TWEENE M.Dan. Featly, OPO-
NENT, AND D. Smith THE
younger, *Respondent*, (now by the Pope intitu-
luled Bishop of *Chalcedon*, and Ordinary of all *England*) at *Paris*. *Sept*.4. 1612. *Stylo nouo*,
touching the Reall presence in the
Sacrament.

LONDON,
Printed by *Felix Kyngston* for *Robert Milbourne*, and
are to be sold at his shop in *Pauls* Churchyard at the
signe of the Greyhound. 1630.

Title page of the account of the disputation between Featley and Smith prepared by John Pory and Ben Jonson.

discourses" which were against one of the rules. Featley "was bound by the Law onely to oppose," Pory wrote, "and D. Smith onely to give his answers, which are here truly set downe, most of them out of his owne writing, as wee depose, who were present at this Disputation." Ben Jonson also signed a statement to the effect that the narrative account and the quotations "are true out of my examination. And of the rest I remember the most, or all: neither can I suspect any part." This suggests that Pory wrote the pamphlet and submitted it to Jonson for examination.[74]

Padua and Turin

In the early summer of 1613 Pory visited Padua and Turin in northeastern Italy "with purpose to see those parts," as Sir Dudley Carleton wrote, "but wants *primum necessarium.*" He further reported that Pory "conjured me with these words—*by the kind and constant intelligence which passeth betwixt you and my best friends in London*—to send him fourteen doubloons, wherewith to disengage him, where he lies in pawn, not knowing how to go forward or backward. I have done more in respect of his friends than himself, for I fear he is fallen too much in love with the pot to be

74. The Protestant version of the disputation may be found in Dan. Featly, *The Grand Sacrilege of the Church of Rome, In taking away the sacred Cup from the Laiety at the Lords Table* (London, 1630). The report by Pory and Jonson is printed in the same volume with a separate title page as *The Summe and Substance of A Disputation Between M. Dan. Featly, Oponent, and D. Smith the younger, Respondent, (now by the Pope intitutuled Bishop of Chalcedon, and Ordinary of all England) at Paris. Sept. 4, 1612. Stylo novo, touching the Real presence in the Sacrament*, pp. 285–306. The Roman Catholic point of view is presented in *The Relection of a Conference Touching the Reall Presence. Or A Bachelours Censure of a Masters Apologie for Doctour Featlie* (Douay, 1636), in which one section is entitled "The Summe of a Conference Betwixt M. D. Smith now B. of Chalcedon, and M. Dan Featly Minister. About the Real Presence." William D. Briggs, in "On Certain Incidents in Ben Jonson's Life," *Modern Philology* 11 (October, 1913):279–88, examines the authorship of the relation of the disputation published in 1630 and concludes "that Pory wrote the pamphlet in consultation with Jonson, who, besides giving him some advice, examined his work and certified to its accuracy." In 1625 Smith became the one Roman Catholic bishop permitted by King James in England; as Bishop of Chalcedon he visited every part of the country, but he later was suspended by the Pope (M. D. R. Leys, *Catholics in England, 1559–1829* [London, 1961], pp. 70–71). In his letter of 19 December 1628 to the Reverend Joseph Mead, Pory reported, "On Wednesday a proclamation was published against one Smyth, a Popish priest, being a Mountibank titular Bishop of Chalcedon, and having amongst a company of geese in Lancashire appeared in his Pontificalibus wth his horned myter and crooked crosier, and having sought to drawe some Idiots from his majesty's alleageance."

much esteemed, and have sent him what he wrote for by Matthew, the post."[75]

Constantinople

From Italy, sometime after July 1613, Pory went on to Constantinople where he became attached to the embassy of Paul Pindar of the Levant Company. He probably went by ship, as he later mentioned in a letter of 4 December 1631 to Viscount Scudamore that he had once visited Messina in Sicily. He remained in Turkey until late in 1616, so long in fact, that his old friend Lord Carew wrote Sir Thomas Roe that "it was long reported in England that he had died in Constantinople." In Constantinople, however, Pory was busy with the affairs of the company. English cloth, tin, lead, and furs were sent out; and raw silk, mohair, drugs and dyes, cotton wool and yarn, spices, figs, dates, indigo, coffee, and Turkish carpets sent home. So favorable a balance of trade developed that the Levant Company became the envy of others. The embassy at Pera, the foreign quarter of the Turkish city, occupied "a faire house within a large field and pleasant gardens compassed with a wall."[76]

It was while he was in Constantinople that Pory translated King James's book, *Déclaration du . . . Roy Jacques . . . pour le droit des Rois et indépendance de leurs Couronnes, contre la harangue d' l'illustrissime Cardinal du Perron*, from French into Italian to please sig. Almorò Nani, the Venetian ambassador there. This book, which had been published in 1615 in London in both French and Latin, grew out of the earlier disagreement between the king and Cardinal du Perron concerning the English oath of allegiance. An oath proposed in France, based on England's, was opposed by the Roman Catholic clergy for whom the cardinal was spokesman.[77] Pory had been entrusted with delivering a treatise on this

75. Edward D. Neill, *History of the Virginia Company of London with Letters to and from the Colony Never Before Printed* (Albany, N.Y., 1896), pp. 135–36.

76. Alexander Brown, *The Genesis of the United States* (Boston, 1890), 2:970; Michael J. Brown, *Itinerant Ambassador, The Life of Sir Thomas Roe* (Lexington, Ky., 1970), pp. 119–20; Alfred C. Wood, *A History of the Levant Company* (Oxford, 1935), p. 238. It is interesting that Pory's exact contemporary, William Strachey (1572–1621), had been in Constantinople in 1606 where he was associated with the British embassy, and like Pory, he was later secretary in Virginia (S. G. Culliford, *William Strachey, 1572–1621* [Charlottesville, Va., 1965], pp. 61–128).

77. King James appears to have employed Pierre du Moulin, a French Protestant, to write this book to which he appended his own name. Du Moulin was honored with the degree of doctor of divinity by Cambridge as well as other benefits

subject when he went to Paris early in 1612. Henry Bertie, who was in Constantinople, had a copy of Pory's recent Italian translation to be delivered in Venice, but he was betrayed by a servant. Bertie was imprisoned by the Inquisition at Ancona but later transferred to Rome where he was eventually released.[78]

Even though he was more or less isolated at his post in Constantinople, Pory played a part in at least one of the many minor struggles for power and position in which ambitious Englishmen then frequently engaged. Both Sir Dudley Carleton and Sir Henry Wotton were attempting to gain favor with the king in order to secure an appointment as ambassador to France. At the peak of the struggle Carleton was unfortunately at the embassy in Venice and thus at a disadvantage, but Wotton was in England. At Easter, 1614, Wotton went to Ware Park to visit John Chamberlain, who was a newsletter writer for Carleton but a friend of both Wotton and Carleton as well as of Pory. Chamberlain grew tired of hearing Wotton talk of "his employment for Fraunce, when as God knowes how long he may linger after it." Pory seems to have recently written Chamberlain something favorable of Carleton or perhaps derogatory of Wotton, because Chamberlain later wrote Carleton, "Having Master Pories discourse there with me, and making some mention of it by chaunce, he [Wotton] was with child till he had seen it, and though I made it somwhat daintie, yet I meant to choake him with it, indeed it put him to silence all the day after. Touching the printing of it, you need not doubt, for there was never any such purpose but only spoken merely."[79]

In November 1616 there were rumors in official circles that Paul Pindar was about to be recalled from Constantinople, and consequently things might come "ill to passe for poor Master Porie."[80] On 18 January 1617 Chamberlain reported to Carleton that "Master Porie is returned from Constantinople and hath ben at White-hall with Secretarie Winwood."[81] Pory undoubtedly was

---

(D. Harris Willson, *King James VI and I* [New York, 1956], pp. 241–42). The work went through several editions in both English and French in London, Paris, and elsewhere (Pollard and Redgrave, *Short-title Catalogue*, nos. 14367–71; *Catalogue Général des Livres Imprimés de la Bibliothèque Nationale* [Paris, 1922], 76:563).

78. Smith, *Life and Letters of Sir Henry Wotton*, 2:111, 114.

79. Chamberlain to Carleton, 12 May 1614, in McClure, *Letters of John Chamberlain*, 1:529. For other accounts of personal maneuvering for position in embassy posts, see Stoye, *English Travellers Abroad, 1604–1667*, pp. 133–74.

80. Chamberlain to Carleton, 23 November 1616, in McClure, *Letters of John Chamberlain*, 2:40.

81. Ibid., 2:50.

reporting what he knew of affairs at Constantinople. His letter of 20 October 1616 to Carleton related that he had been chosen by the English merchants resident at Constantinople to make such a report. The minutes of the meeting of the General Court of the Levant Company at the home of Governor Sir Thomas Lowe on 16 January 1617 recorded that "letters of the 5th of November from the Ambassadour and nation in Constantinople, were now read and considered of, and Mr. Pory the bearer was heard at large for such business as was given him, instructions from the Ambassador whereof he made pticulir relation and delivered in what uncertaine state the Naton now lived there by reason of sundry oppressions and wrongs offered by the Grand Signior and his officers of which it was hoped the kinges late letters would procure some remedy." In a letter of 10 April 1617, signed by sixteen members of the Levant Company, Pindar was informed of the receipt of the information he had sent by Pory.[82]

Sometime between 1613 and 1620, but undoubtedly quite soon after his return from Constantinople, Pory presented two printed Chinese books and a Persian manuscript of Divan by Hafiz, the fourteenth-century lyric poet, to the library at Oxford. Each of the three volumes bears the contemporary notation that they were the gift of John Pory, armiger, but there is no evidence, such as marginal notations, that he had read or otherwise used them. While he was in Constantinople, Pory also purchased books for Sir Henry Saville, warden of Merton College, Oxford, and Carleton's father-in-law.[83]

About the middle of July 1617 Sir Dudley Carleton, then ambassador at The Hague, began an attempt to find a suitable secretary for the embassy. He seems also to have had John Chamberlain on the watch for a person, because on 19 July Chamberlain wrote,

> I cannot yet bethincke myself of any fit man for your turne but
> Master Pory, who hath leysure enough for ought I see, and not long
> since he had a meaning to make a journy to you, and desired I wold
> procure him a pacquet or some other employment to beare his
> charge. I did what he required, but either he hath chaunged his
> minde, or els is not so hastie as he made shew of, for he speakes no

82. Public Record Office. S.P. 105/147/86–87; S.P. 105/110/88.
83. Falconer Madan and H. H. E. Craster, *A Summary Catalogue of Western Manuscripts in the Bodleian Library at Oxford* (Oxford, 1922), 2:543. When Pindar returned to England in 1620, he also presented Arabian and Persian manuscripts to the library (Wood, *A History of the Levant Company*, pp. 84, 242; and Lee, *Dudley Carleton to John Chamberlain*, pp. 177–78).

Sir Paul Pindar ... Anno 1614. Constantinop^s.

Sir Paul Pindar, Pory's employer in Constantinople from 1613 to 1617.

Tommaso Bertelè, Il Palazzo Degli Ambasciatori di Venezia a Constantinopoli
(Bologna, 1932)

Bust of Almorò Nani in the Church of San Giobbe, Venice. Nani was the Venetian agent in Constantinople from 1614 to 1620 for whom Pory translated King James's Déclaration *into Italian.*

Tommaso Bertelee, Il Palazzo Degli Ambasciatori di Venezia a Constantinopoli
(Bologna, 1932)

*Pera (foreground), the foreign section of Constantinople, about
1600.*

more of it. I have not seen him since I received your letter, but
when I do I will spur him on to the journy, without any word of
what you have written, and when you have him there you may do
with him as you see cause. In the mean time if I can light on any
other I will geve you notice.[84]

Carleton replied that Pory would be very welcome on two
conditions, first that he give up any idea of returning to Constantinople, and second that he give up "the pot (which is hard in this
country)." He insisted that Chamberlain "treat with him upon the
point . . . and if he takes this course, you may assure him of good
usage."[85]

On 27 August Chamberlain wrote Carleton from his home
at Ware Park:

Touching Master Pory I can promise nothing till my going back to
London, which I know not how long it wilbe before the terme: he
shall not want any counsaile or incouragement that I can geve him,
as likewise I did spurre him what I could toward his pretended
journy into those parts, only upon my opinion it might be to goode
purpose both for himself and you. But the last time I spake with
him I perceved that he had ben put in hope of some employment
there [in London] for the marchants, which fayling, he was no

84. McClure, *Letters of John Chamberlain,* 2:87.
85. Carleton to Chamberlain, 22 August 1617, in Birch, *Court and Times of
James I,* 2:29.

more forward in the viage, and yet mee thought he lingered more then ordinarie still about me, which made mee suspect he had somwhat els to say which I was nothing willing to heare.[86]

The Hague

Pory, without knowing that Carleton was considering employing him as secretary at the embassy, finally was persuaded to visit The Hague. Chamberlain procured some dispatches from the Foreign Office for Pory to deliver to the embassy,[87] and early in September he took a ship for Amsterdam on what Carleton described as "somewhat a long voyage." After Pory had his packet, Carleton continued, he had to remain in London from Wednesday until Monday "for want of wings, there being no money to pay the post." Once underway, however, he lost no time in making the trip, and in Amsterdam took advantage of the opportunity to see the new 1200-ton ship built there after an English model for the Knights of Malta. Soon after Pory joined Carleton, however, it appeared to his host that he was in great haste to be on his way again, "having too many irons in the fire to think of any settled course in this place." Carleton, seeing Pory's impatience to be off again, said nothing to him about the secretary's position at the embassy, deciding instead to "have patience until I may be fitted to mind."[88]

Pory seems to have left The Hague in early October. On the eighteenth of the month Chamberlain wrote Carleton that "Master Pory appeares not neither can I learne of any body that he is returned." Two weeks later, however, he wrote, "I met yesterday with Master Pory who related at large to me the kind usage he found with you. I seemed to marvayle how he could leave you, but I perceve by him that the least whistling may call him again, and to say the truth he did intimate as much."[89]

Carleton's interest in Pory continued. In November he enclosed a letter for Pory in one to Chamberlain with the request that it be conveyed "speedily unto him, he being lodged in the Strand,

86. McClure, *Letters of John Chamberlain*, 2:97.
87. *Collections of the Massachusetts Historical Society* (Boston, 1871), 9:12–13.
88. Carleton to Chamberlain, 12 Sept. 1617, in Birch, *Court and Times of James I*, 2:32–33; Lee, *Dudley Carleton to John Chamberlain*, p. 244.
89. McClure, *Letters of John Chamberlain*, 2:103, 112.

A typical Low Country scene in 1605, such as Pory may have passed through on his visits to the Continent.

but I know not where, save only by description, at the next house where Sir Barnard Dewhurst died."[90]

Pory's next employment after his return from visiting Sir Dudley at The Hague lasted only briefly, but it took him to the Continent again. The Privy Council employed Pory and several other men to go in search of William Cecil, Lord Roos, grandson of Thomas Cecil, first Earl of Exeter. Roos, who had become a Roman Catholic, had been on uncommonly friendly terms with the Spanish ambassador, Don Diego Sarmiento de Acuna, Count Gondomar, and was suspected of having revealed information to him which

90. Carleton to Chamberlain, 8 November 1617, in Birch, *Court and Times of James I,* 2:52.

should have been denied him in his position of ambassador.[91] Court rumor had it that Lord Roos, with Gondomar's aid, had escaped and made his way to Rome where "he was received with distinguished honor by the sovereign pontiff."[92] The search was not successful, and Chamberlain informed Carleton on 14 February 1618 that "Master Pory is come backe. I met with him two dayes since, and he will not be acknowne that he was farther then Turin and the south parts of Fraunce whether he wold seeme to have some employment: he talkes much of Master Wake, what credit he is in, what a port and table he kepes more like an ambassador then an Agent, and that he is in such favor with the Duke that he will do nothing without him."[93]

Later in 1618 Pory again visited Sir Dudley, and this time he was invited to become a member of the embassy staff. Something—perhaps it was only his restless spirit—kept Pory from accepting. On 14 October 1618 Chamberlain wrote Carleton, "I met this day with Master Poorie, but in such a pickle that I perceve the pot and he are so fast friends that they cannot easilie be parted. He stammered out somewhat how loth he was to leave you, but that he was tired [sic] in honestie I know not to whom, with much other like matter, but the conclusion was that I finde he wishes he had continued with you, and I thincke you might have him for the whistling if he were worth it."[94]

Pory again left Sir Dudley after a brief visit as he had the year before. His reason, as Chamberlain had guessed earlier, was "some employment . . . for the marchants." In his letter to Carleton on 25 October 1618 Pory apologized, "I had reason to make haste out of the lowe countires, to give my lo: Riche,[95] the speediest and best satisfaction I coulde, seeing his lordship upon his honour had promised me at the returne of his ships anything riche, £500 for his share, besides what I coulde gett from his parteners. And therfor (good my lord) thinke not amisse of me, though I tooke my leave of your lordship some what abruptly."

91. Godfrey Goodman, *The Court of James the First* (London, 1839), 1:182.
92. *Collections of the Massachusetts Historical Society*, 9:13; G. P. V. Akrigg, *Jacobean Pageant, or The Court of King James I* (Cambridge, Mass., 1963), pp. 273–74.
93. McClure, *Letters of John Chamberlain*, 2:139 (Isaac Wake [1580?–1632] was English agent to the Duke of Savoy at Turin).
94. Ibid., 2:171.
95. Sir Robert Rich (1587–1658) soon succeeded his father as Earl of Warwick.

In spite of his almost constant search for employment Pory's primary profession, if it may be so called, was that of newsletter writer or "intelligencer," to which he seems always to have turned when there was no other business to occupy his time and replenish his purse. Pory was one of several active newsletter writers at the time of the appearance of regular printed newspapers in England, and he continued to serve his patrons almost until his death. He never felt that the printed news offered a serious threat to the personally tailored service that he offered but instead urged at least one of his patrons to read the printed news as well as the newsletters that he sent.

Men who spent only a portion of their time in London were anxious not to lose touch with affairs of the court and to know the current gossip of the city. Some who remained in London relied on newsletter writers for the same kind of news, of course, but they also found the foreign news of interest. Newsletters were often passed around among the recipient's friends.

Men in positions of authority or with ambition for such a position engaged the services of professional newsletter writers who gathered the news and forwarded it by regular or special courier. These news correspondents, of whom John Chamberlain, Thomas Locke, and John Pory are considered to have been among the most able, helped create an atmosphere that led to the establishment of the printed newspaper in England.[96] Because of Pory's lengthy news-filled letters from Virginia it has even been suggested that the "evolution of the newspaper in the United States . . . technically starts with John Pory."[97] On 2 December 1620 Pieter van den Keere in Amsterdam issued the first known printed news in English.[98] Perhaps some time in the same year, and continuing as late as September 1621, Thomas Archer published a paper in London, but no copies are known.[99]

Forward-looking men in London recognized the potential

---

96. *Times* (London), *Tercentenary Handlist of English & Welsh Newspapers, Magazines & Reviews, 1620–1920* (London, 1920), p. 6.

97. *Encyclopaedia Britannica*, 14th ed., s.v. "Newspapers, United States" (James Melvin Lee, who wrote this article, was director of the Department of Journalism, New York University).

98. Joseph Frank, *The Beginnings of the English Newspaper, 1620–1660* (Cambridge, Mass., 1961), p. 3.

99. Folke Dahl, *A Bibliography of English Corantos, Periodicals and Newsbooks, 1620–1642* (London, 1952), pp. 49–50.

significance of the printed news in English if it were issued regularly. Among the State Papers in the Public Record Office is an undated and unsigned memorandum of about 1621 which has been attributed to Thomas Locke.[100] It contains an intriguing proposal for printing a newspaper and for other purposes, and although Pory was then in Virginia he must have known of the plan as his name was included as one of the petitioners. "My suit is," the petition reads, "that your lordship wold geve me leave to be a sutor to the King that Mr. Porey and my self may procurr a patent to be overseers of all books of humanity which shall be printed, that he will geve unto us a fee of £20 per annum to each of us for our paynes, and with all to geve us leave to print a Gazette or weekly occurants which we shall gett from other parts, that none may print them without our lycence & for this we wold give his Majesty as much rent as he shall geve us for overseeing books for £20 a year more, for which we may have a patent of that to us or our assigns."

By way of pleading their cause and convincing officials to grant them what they sought, the unknown petitioner, speaking for himself and Pory, made three interesting proposals:

> 1 To settle a way when there shalbe any revolt or back slyding in matters of religion or obedience (which comonly growes with rumors among the vulgar) to draw them in by the same lynes that drew them out by spreeding amongst them such reports as may best make for that matter to which we wold have them drawne.
>
> 2 To establish a speedy and reddy way wherby to disperse into the veynes of the whole body of a state such matter as may best temper it, & be most agreeable to the disposition of the head & the principale members, upon all occasions that shalbe offred.
>
> 3 To devise meanes to raise the spiritts of the people and to quicken ther concepts & undoubtedly to guage their tastes of matters clericle from the common mire of worldliness. It makes such apt to be drawn from the cold sodish humor of sloth & extends the sense by degrees to the conceipt of the right rules of reason, wherby they ar wrought easily to obey those which by those rules shall comand them.
>
> Of this ancient tymes affords many precedents & for moderne we see these to be the causes sending these Gazetts weekly as from the centre of newes to disperse all occurants to all parts of the world.

100. Mary Anne Everett Green, ed., *Calendar of State Papers, Domestic Series, of the Reign of James I, 1619–1623* (London, 1858), p. 330; *Times (London), Tercentenary Handlist,* p. 7.

This sells mercurius Gallobelgicus now in Germany the advisoes in France & the Novellas in Italy and Spayne. In which point noe country is so heavy as our brittayn, which I have heard reproved in forayn parts for the negligence heerin. From Anworpe Brussells Hage Colloyn Francford Prage Vienna Gratz Venice Florence Rome Naples Genoa Spayne Paris & Lyons we have the occurrances every week in all places of the world yes even heer amongst us britans. In all these places or provincies the ploughman and artisan can talk of thes matters and mabe both benefitt and reeveared by knowing them. Why shold our Brittaynes be more muddy then all the world not to conceipt or aprehend thes matters & make the same use of them that others doe. Much good may come to the state generally by thes means for the reasons allegded before and they shal serve for a pretext of the use which I will propose though to say the truth it is my own particular benefitt that is the gretest mover to me in that matter.

The petition closed with the promise that "if this might be gotte it wold be worth unto me £200 per ann and . . . I shold alwas keep an historical preserve allwase ready of what soever shold passe in the world."[101]

The memorandum apparently was given by Locke to his employer, Sir Dudley Carleton, who was the "lordship" to whom it was first submitted. Sir Dudley presumably passed the memorandum on to the secretary of state, but there is no indication that any action was ever taken in spite of the fact that somewhere along its route of travel it was revised, certain sections were deleted and rewritten, and other parts were numbered to indicate a different sequence than in the draft as it was first drawn up.[102]

Pory's newsletters began at a time before the printed newspaper appeared in England, of course, but before his death in 1636 more than a dozen different ones had been published. Pory referred to some of the printed "gazettes" or "corantos" several times, notably in his letters of late October 1632, after they had been suppressed by decree of Star Chamber. The men who subscribed to Pory's service were thereby able to read the latest court gossip as well as the doings of royalty and others up and down the social scale—information not yet to be found in the printed news. He also

101. Unsigned, undated memorandum. Public Record Office, S.P. 14/124/360. See also, Green, *Calendar of State Papers, 1619–1623*, p. 330; and *Times (London), Tercentenary Handlist*, pp. 6–7.

102. *Times (London), Tercentenary Handlist*, p. 7; J. B. Williams [pseud. for for Joseph George Middiman], *A History of English Journalism to the Foundation of the Gazette* (London, 1908), pp. 23–24.

included a variety of other topics, such as the latest reports on the wars in Europe, which might also be found in the printed news.

Humor, proverbs, and clever expressions mark much of Pory's writing. These sometimes suffer when taken out of context, but a few will bear repeating: a disgrace at home to an ambassador after he had arrived in England, Pory wrote on 8 September 1631 "will (I suppose) put water into his wine, and will a little curbe the fierceness of his spirite." On 12 January 1632: "it is as easy for him to gett a penny [from a certain person], as to wring Hercules clubb out of his fiste." Some pirates who had been captured by a group of merchants, he reported on 15 November 1632 in a classic example of understatement, "were entertained according to their quality."

When Queen Henrietta Maria's troublesome French servants refused to obey the king's orders to leave England, King Charles issued new orders that they were to be thrown out into the street. The servants took the hint and departed, and Pory carefully charted their progress toward the channel. They finally reached Dover, he said, "from whence God send them a faire winde." The following week, 17 August 1626, after writing a letter filled with bits of insignificant information on numerous subjects, he concluded, "Now for offending your sight I will sewe no more patches upon the beggers cloke, but will cut the thred of this motley discourse."

Numerous apt quotations, many of them in French or Latin and occasionally in Spanish, mark Pory's letters. A few of the words he used might be considered offensive today, but they apparently were commonly used in the seventeenth century and certainly served the purpose in making a point in the context in which they were used. Some of his classical quotations, although not always entirely accurate, came from the Roman writers Cicero, Horace, Lucan, Pliny, Seneca, Suetonius, Terence, and Vergil. His studies at Cambridge obviously were remembered, or perhaps he always had his old commonplace book close at hand.

Many letters which Pory wrote must have been destroyed. He specifically asked one of his patrons to burn his letters; a practice, he mentioned, that some of his other correspondents already followed. Several original letters known to Thomas Birch in the nineteenth century can no longer be located.[103] There are

103. In the 1890s an estate agent "burned up a lot of old trash," as it was then described, at Charlecote, and villagers later recalled seeing what appeared to be Elizabethan parchments being destroyed. Others remembered that in their youth old letters from the gatehouse at Charlecote had been used by local shops to wrap sweets. Sir Thomas Lucy, one of the men to whom Pory wrote, lived at Charlecote (Lady Fairfax-Lucy to William S. Powell, 20 May 1948).

references in Pory's surviving letters to others that he wrote to various people but which cannot now be found. The specific periods during which he was employed as a newsletter writer can be determined only in a general way because only scattered letters exist for a part of the time. In 1606 and 1612 he wrote to Sir Robert Cotton, in 1610 to Sir Ralph Winwood, and in 1613 to Sir Thomas Edmondes. Because of the gaps, however, it is impossible to say with certainty whether he was employed by these men or whether he was simply writing personal letters. The nature of their contents, however, suggests that they were newsletters. While at Constantinople with Ambassador Paul Pindar, Pory began to correspond at length with Sir Dudley Carleton. From 1619 to 1622, when he was in Virginia, he often wrote to Sir Edwin Sandys, treasurer of the Virginia Company, informing him in some detail of affairs in the colony. Letters survive for the period between 1625 and 1630 addressed to the Reverend Joseph Mead. Pory's last employer was Sir Thomas Puckering, whose sole claim to fame seems to be that he was an active politician who held no important office save that of companion to Prince Henry. Letters to Puckering date between 1630 and 1633, but during 1631 to 1632 he wrote with regularity to John, Viscount Scudamore, and from this employment more letters survive than to any of the others.

Pory observed regular writing days for his patrons and felt in conscience bound to explain any deviation. He once explained a delay in writing as being due to "my forced being away upon the writing day." On another occasion he wrote, "The next Thursday being so near Christmas day, I must crave pardon for not writing." Once illness prevented him from writing to Lord Scudamore. Thursday was mentioned as the writing day to Puckering, but Saturday was reserved for Scudamore's letter. With rare exception, letters were written at weekly intervals.

Only two references survive to indicate the pay that Pory received for his efforts. Lord Scudamore paid him at the end of each six months, a total of £20 for the year. Pory gently reminded his patron at the expiration of the first period in a postscript, "I began to write unto you the first Satturday in December and this is the last Satturday of May: wherby it appears I have served your lordship full 6. moneths. Whereupon what your lordship wilbe pleased to inferre, I shall humbly expect." On 16 June 1632 he wrote, "I understand there are two of your lordships servants in towne, who have sought me at Butters shop, with whom as yet it hath not bene my good hap to meet. I make no doubt, but they intend good toward mee, and doe hope I shall see them ere night."

In addition to payment for his regular newsletters, Pory also sold his patrons copies of "excellent discourses" which he copied from various sources available to him in London. The speech of Sir Benjamin Rudyerd, 28 April 1628, may have been such an item. On 22 September 1631, in a postscript to a regular letter to Sir Thomas Puckering (which was also shared with Sir Thomas Lucy), he offered for ten shillings each an assortment of "discourses" by Mons. de Rohan, a "character" of Cardinal Richelieu, an "apology" of the cardinal, and "a pathetical Remonstrance" of the princes assembled before the Holy Roman Emperor in Leipzig. Lucy agreed to share the cost of these with Puckering. Several pieces which must have been prepared in this category are included among Pory's letters: the Rudyerd speech of 28 April 1628; Dr. Mainwaring's submission, 21 June 1628; the king's speech to both houses, 26 June 1628; "Certain speeches whereof one Mr. Melvin a Scottishman is accused," 26 June 1628; and "A true recital of what hath passed," 30 October 1630. Similar handwritten reports, especially speeches made in Parliament, had been prepared for sale since the middle of Queen Elizabeth's reign.[104]

Pory spent most of his time while he was in London in the City—that section around St. Paul's. The Reverend Joseph Mead addressed Pory once in care of his sister in Aldermanbury; another time he was living in the Strand. The apothecary shop of Ralph Yeardley (brother of the Virginia governor, Sir George) in Wood Street was a convenient place to leave and pick up messages and parcels. For business purposes, however, he made the printshop of Nathaniel Butter and Nicholas Bourne in Watling Street his headquarters. It was here that Lord Scudamore's servants left his pay. Butter and Bourne were the pioneer newspaper publishers in England, and they received news from abroad which they translated and published. Pory quite clearly drew much of the foreign news which he related in his own newsletters from sources which they supplied. In return he probably shared local news with Butter and Bourne. Pory perhaps also helped with the translation of foreign news for which he may have been paid.

In his manuscript newsletters Pory was generally careful to refer to his sources except for the most general information. Frequently his remarks were prefaced by such statements as, "It was tolde me also by a Courrier at Whitehall . . . ," "A scholer of Cambridge writes to me . . . ," "Dr. Rivers the kinges Advocate on

---

104. Frank, *The Beginnings of the English Newspaper, 1620–1660*, pp. 19–20.

Sunday was sennight told a noble friend of mine that . . . ," "I was tolde by a noble Cavalier that an Herald shewed him under my lord high Constables hand . . . ," "The relation which Sir Abraham agent of the Queen of Bohemia gave me . . . ," "One Mr Slanning, sonne in lawe to Sir James Bagg of Plymouth, who (as I heard partly from his owne mouth, and partly from others that heard him speak as well as myself) said . . . ," "I have heard from the mouth of a gentleman newly returned from Spaine (who conversed there with the Duke of Lennox) that . . . ," "My lord Wimbledon and Sir William Curtyn tolde a friend of mine yesterday . . . ," or "I heard John Tredescant tell my lord of C[anterbury] that. . . . "

Not only did he make an attempt to indicate the sources of his information, but he sometimes also appraised its trustworthiness. By such statements as, "These two stories, though I heard confirmed [by] many, yet I will leave them to a fortnights probation," "Yet can I skarce beleeve what one tolde me to day," "Some are of opinion (though I am not) that . . . ," or "a certain intelligent Dutchman, a friend of mine, telles me a thing which I hold (if not a monster) a Paradie at the least," he cautioned his reader to judge for himself whether to believe the report.

Grist for his newsletter mill, which sometimes produced two or three different letters each week, was collected from other sources than Butter and Bourne's foreign packets. Pory spent much of each day at the Exchange or in St. Paul's Walk where crowds gathered to buy and sell and to discuss affairs of the day. Mealtime in nearby taverns also drew knowledgeable people together, and Pory was not above joining a group of diners for the opportunity of picking up bits of information. Some of the tavern patrons were employees of great men, and their egos were flattered when they were questioned about the activity of persons of high rank. And Pory knew a host of the great men themselves. These he encountered on his frequent trips down to Whitehall or on such semipublic occasions as the masques or progresses. Dudley Carleton commented in 1607 that before Pory completed preparation for a projected trip abroad, he took solemn leave of Prince Henry, assorted lords and ladies, "and all the ambassadors."[105] Sometimes he was the dinner guest of the Archbishop of Canterbury, the Lord Mayor, or others in high position. He was, himself, called upon by important men for the information he could furnish them. Ambassadors Carleton, Carew, and Pindar, Secretary Winwood, Lord Rich, and others whose names occur with considerable regularity

105. Lee, *Dudley Carleton to John Chamberlain*, p. 96.

throughout his letters were his confidants, and both they and he benefited from the association.

There are enough of Pory's letters written within a short space of time to several people to suggest that he did not simply send the same letter to each of his patrons as did some of the other newsletter writers. Instead, he tailored each letter to the interests of the person to whom it was written. In some instances, when the same basic information was given to more than one person, different details were emphasized. That Pory enjoyed his work is evident from the enthusiasm which he often revealed, but he also expressed his satisfaction quite openly. "I take delight" in writing newsletters, he told Lord Scudamore in March 1632. Later in the year, when his patron, perhaps in anticipation of an appointment to a post in Paris, decided to end his subscription to the newsletters, Pory commented, "One's will is the horse he rides until he dies," intimating that he intended to continue to write newsletters for so long as he lived.

In an age when a man, or a woman for that matter, might be thrown into prison and held there for years for the slightest intimation of anything offensive to those in power, Pory wrote very frankly. He clearly knew the minds of his patrons, however, and felt secure in their confidence. On 17 December 1631, as he was beginning to correspond with Lord Scudamore, he cautioned him that he hoped "your lordship will (as other mine honorable patrones use to doe) comitte all the letters I have or shall write to you, to the safest secretary in the world, the fire." This suggestion Pory repeated the following March after writing in a particularly frank manner about an outburst which had just occurred in Parliament between Lord Powis and Sir John Finch. "These thinges I presume to write for your lordships contente," he said, "and therfore doe hope you love mee so well as to burne my letters always, when you have perused them." Since he often quoted directly from persons of high rank, Pory placed himself in a position of considerable jeopardy, considering the uncertainty of the times, but he was clearly an advocate of the *freedom of the press*—whether it be in manuscript or printed form. After a decree of Star Chamber on 17 October 1632 stopped the publication of the curantos, he observed that "written newes must needs now be the welcomer," and there is no evidence that he changed the pattern of reporting which he had pursued for years. Just ten days after the decree he remarked, "This stoppage is no cure for their woundes, it's but a palliation; and truth will burst out and manifest itselfe." But it was not until 1638, two years after Pory's death, that his friends Butter and Bourne were permitted to resume publication of the news.

The range of subjects covered by Pory during his life as an active writer of newsletters is nearly endless. Political maneuvering and war must head the list of popular topics, as they were subjects of peculiar interest to his clients. So were the social activities in London and the country. Voyages of discovery were mentioned as he heard of them, along with reports of travelers returned from abroad. Freaks of nature, storms, comets, ambergris from the sea off Cornwall, pirates, robbers, murder, funerals, public executions, mercantile activity, duels, illness, and an extensive list of additional subjects might be said to characterize many of Pory's letters. Nearly every letter contained a variety of information. He mentioned people of high and low estate, sometimes in very personal terms. He reported on one occasion that the king had slept with the queen for two nights in succession (which, considering the morals of the time, might have been worthy of note), and again he recorded that an ill lord had had an enema, after which he steadily improved from the effects of a fall from his horse! Pory frequently made passing comments about some of the literary figures of the day. Ben Jonson, Inigo Jones, and John Donne were particularly well known to him. The poets Michael Drayton, Hugh Holland, and Sir John Suckling were mentioned; playwrights Aurelian Townsend, Walter Montagu, William D'Avenant, and Francis Fane were deemed worthy of observation. The artist, Peter Rubens, also entered into Pory's vision. In addition to remarks about the activity of scores of well-known men and women, he also related the doings of countless lesser persons, many of whom now defy identification. Some were carriers of the post, servants, messengers, soldiers, tavern keepers, or ship captains; others were printers, actors, scholars, clergymen, merchants, military officers, sons and daughters of the gentry, or simply random friends and acquaintances of the men to whom he was writing, few of whom made a lasting imprint in the records of the time. He also wrote about the theatre, plays and masques, and new books. He managed to pick up news from Virginia, Hudson's River, New England, and Canada, or news relating to the Caribbean Islands. News from the Continent, of course, was commonplace, but he spiced it with news of the Orient. India, Turkey, and Russia were sometimes mentioned, and the return of a two-year expedition in search of the Northwest Passage was commented upon.

Pory himself, in many respects, is almost as elusive as some of the people about whom he wrote. Except for a few official records, scattered comments by a handful of friends such as Sir Dudley Carleton, John Chamberlain, and John Donne, and what can be deduced about him from his own letters, little can be said with confidence about what kind of person he was. It seems safe to presume, by the nature of his work, that he was a friendly and outgoing man with an inquiring mind. He had a splendid memory, recalling in later years a number of seemingly insignificant events of thirty or more years before.

For about a dozen years in middle life Pory had a problem with strong drink. This was first mentioned in 1607 while he was in London as a member of Parliament. John Chamberlain wrote to Dudley Carleton on 13 February that Sir Edward Hoby of Bisham, Berkshire, had had "a great feast" which Pory attended, but that he returned home "prettelie well whitled." Six years later Chamberlain again commented on Pory's weakness: "I hear he is fallen too much in love with the pot." In August 1613, a few weeks later, he advised Carleton that he "had not need meet with many such mothes as Master Poorie who must have both meat and monie, for drinke he will find out for himself if it be above ground or no deeper then the cellar, and this I had from his best friends as he termes them." In early November Carleton wrote to Chamberlain from Padua that Pory, "I think, is settled here for this winter and, if he behave himself no otherwise then he hath done hitherto, he might surely have challenged of his friends at Paris a better report for I find him no ways disordered." But even while Carleton was writing, Pory was brought in so drunk that he could not stand up, and Carleton crossed through the words *for I find him no ways disordered* in the letter before him.

Pory evidently had been trying to conquer his weakness and initially made a good impression on Carleton, but the ease with which wine could be had in Padua proved too great a temptation. His determination persisted, however, for in 1617, from The Hague, Carleton expressed a willingness to have Pory as his secretary if he continued steadfast "against the pot (which is hard in this country)." The final reference to a drunken Pory was made by Chamberlain on 14 October 1618 when he noted he had seen Pory that day "in such a pickle that I perceive the pot and he are so fast friends that they cannot easily be parted." Less than two months later, nevertheless, Chamberlain found Pory in a state of great anticipation over the prospects of an appointment as secretary in Virginia; Pory was determined that in Virginia he would become "a sufficient sober man seeing there is no wine in all that climate." And it seems that in this purpose he succeeded. In January 1620, in a letter to Sir Edwin Sandys, Pory discussed the prospects for growing grapes and establishing vineyards in Virginia when he concluded, "But of this subject enough, wherof I have so lardgely dilated, not because I thirst after it; for I thanke god, I drinke water here with as much (if not more) pleasure and content, as I dranke wine in those parts." Afterwards the subject was never mentioned again by either Pory or his friends.[106]

On rare occasions Pory mentioned some illness from which he temporarily suffered. An "accidental coald" in January 1606 briefly affected his hearing. After reaching Jamestown in Virginia in 1619 he wrote that he had had a fever at sea which continued for a few days after he landed; it cleared up quickly, and he soon remarked on the good health that he enjoyed there. On 10 March 1632 he missed a writing day because of an infected left knee, but, as he wrote the next week, "God almighty (whose name be praised for it) provided me a man, who by his skill, method, and assiduity hath cured all." In May of the same year Dr. Theodore Gulston, one of the country's most respected physicians, died of what Pory described as "a long toothake, and an ulcer or gangrene in one of his jawes." He noted that neither the doctor, himself, nor any of the other doctors in London knew how to cure the ailment, yet Pory commented that he had known "an olde woman in the country by her empirick skill cure the like." Unfortunately no records survive to tell the cause of Pory's death just four years hence at the age of sixty-four.

The Pory family had produced several clergymen, and John Pory was a devout Anglican, if judgment may be passed from scattered references in his writing. He wrote reverently of God and those who served Him; he mentioned Christmas holidays and wished his friends a merry Christmas. In his book on Africa he referred to the feast days of the church, and he mentioned "the holy prophet John the Baptist." On the other hand he had no sympathy for Roman Catholics. On 22 September 1631, for example, he wrote of a Roman Catholic military commander who failed to capture a Protestant town which he had expected would be granted to him as a reward. "But God laughed them to scorne, & the holy

106. McClure, *Letters of John Chamberlain*, 1:244, 472; 2:171, 190; Pory to Sandys, 16 January 1620; Lee, *Dudley Carleton to John Chamberlain*, pp. 145, 150, 246. For whatever the evidence may be worth to substantiate this observation, Pory's handwriting remained firm and steady, virtually unchanged, through 1633, when his last-known letter was written at the age of sixty-one. In none of his letters can anything incoherent be detected; instead his conscientious attention to duty is quite clear.

one of Israell had them in derision," Pory commented. He advocated restoration into the Litany of the *Book of Common Prayer* a prayer of King Edward VII's time against the presumed power of the Pope. Another attitude of opposition is also reflected in his reference to "the impious and abominable sects of the Jewes and Mahumetans" in Africa.

Financial problems frequently plagued Pory. He often complained of the lack of funds, and when he was forced to borrow money he worried about repaying it. Sir Dudley Carleton once lent him £20 for a trip to the Continent, and one of Pory's letters hints that he repaid it only after he received a legacy from Sir Walter Cope. Once he hesitated to go on a journey because of the "wante of mony to bringe me backe againe." Before deciding whether to accept the offered appointment as secretary in Virginia he wanted the salary settled, since "I mean not to adventure my Carkase in so dangerous a business for nothing."

Pory was conceited on certain occasions. He sometimes commented that he had found himself in a position of authority over some who might have considered themselves his "betters," as when he was in Turkey on the staff of Paul Pindar or in Jamestown as secretary. On the other hand he was occasionally humble and contrite. "I, whom the crosses & disgraces of the world had so much humbled, as I had not the courage or ambition once to aspire to come into the presence of this prince," he wrote on 16 July 1613 when Victor Amadeus I, prince of the House of Savoy, sought him out in a crowd and engaged him in lengthy conversation. Pory was easily discouraged but quickly cheered by the prospect of improvement. He was not given the position of secretary to Pindar in Turkey, and he was briefly depressed in his lower position. Soon, however, he was reporting new activities and apparently never looked back with regret. He was mildly disappointed at not being selected for a second three-year term as secretary in Virginia, but he set out on a voyage of exploration up and down the coast and soon returned to London where he became involved in Virginia affairs on an even higher plane.

Numerous expressions of respect and regard for the ladies and mistresses of the households of his correspondents mark many of Pory's letters. In some cases the ladies are identified while in others they are not.

Pory died a bachelor, and in none of his surviving letters is there any clear indication of his love for any single lady. Nevertheless it takes only a modest amount of reading between the lines to assume that he was enamored of Isabel ("Bettie") Cope, daughter of his good friend Sir Walter, while he was in London as a member of Parliament. Bettie cried so loudly when Pory was about to leave for the Continent in the summer of 1607 that when she finally stopped, Dudley Carleton commented that she had "put up her pipes."[107] Pory wrote to Carleton on 3 January 1610, "I have no other newyears guift to present you with, but Sir Walter Copes, my ladies, and my Mistresses harty kind commendations, not onely to your selfe, but to your lady." His letter of 17 July to Sir Ralph Winwood concludes, "Sir W. Cope, my Lady & my Mistress are all in good health, & remember their affectionat love & service to your lordship." Although Pory was not in the employ of Cope, he seems to have been in close communication with his household.

Nothing more conclusive than a series of suggestive events can be pointed to on this subject, but on 12 May 1611, soon after the dissolution of Parliament, Pory was licensed to travel abroad and remained away from England for nearly six years. Had he sought the hand of Mistress Isabel Cope and been rejected? Some elusive meaning may lurk behind the words of John Donne's mysterious satire which mentioned both Pory and the Copes, beginning *"Believe in thy havings, and thou hast them."* At any rate, on 30 April 1612, Miss Cope was married to twenty-two-year-old Henry Rich who later became the Earl of Holland, but who ultimately was beheaded. Pory at that time was forty. Some unspecified but clearly unhappy event occurred just before Pory left England, because he later recorded that at the time he was "as a ship without ballaste [and] subjecte to some mens impetuous humours, who sought to sporte themselves with my disgrace." He must have turned instinctively to his good friend, Sir Dudley Carleton, in this time of trouble. Pory recalled this in a letter of 18 December 1614. "I do assure you upon so dreadfull an attestation as the calling of god and his Angelles to witness, that since I last kissed your hande, I never swerved from that wholesome and divine counsill, which your lordship with the most persuasive oratorie of love, sweetness, and tender compassion infused into my then unsetled & distracted mind."[108]

Pory then assured Carleton that he had "conquered all doubtes and difficulties," but since Carleton understood what these were they were not specified. It may have been a mention of Sir Walter Cope by Carleton that brought all of this back to his mind.

107. Lee, *Dudley Carleton to John Chamberlain*, p. 96.
108. Carleton's advice, of course, might well have been related to any one of a number of possible subjects, perhaps even his fondness for wine.

Illustrated London News, *10 August 196*

Cope Castle, Kensington, London, home of Sir Walter Cope. Pory frequently visited and felt very much at home here. The wings on each side were added at a later time, after it came into the possession of Cope's son-in-law, Henry Rich, Earl of Holland and was known as Holland House.

"For the dolefull newes of Sir Walter Copes death," Pory continued, "howe can I chuse but be extreame sorry, whenas in him I have lost absolutely the best friende I had in Englande."

Sir Walter died not many years after completing his large and attractive home, Cope Castle, and he was deeply in debt. His widow was forced to move, and the house eventually went to her son-in-law, Henry Rich.[109] Pory and Lady Cope, nevertheless, continued on friendly terms. In 1615 John Chamberlain relayed some

109. Cope Castle came to be known as Holland House after Rich became the Earl of Holland. In September 1940 the house was gutted by a fire started by German incendiary bombs and stood derelict until the blackened walls were pulled down in 1968 (Derek Hudson, *Holland House in Kensington* [London, 1967], passim; and *Illustrated London News*, 10 August 1968, pp. 15–17. Richard C. Barnett, *Place, Profit, and Power: A Study of the Servants of William Cecil* [Chapel Hill, N.C., 1969], pp. 50–55).

news of him from Sir Dudley Carleton to her. Chamberlain also reported that Sir Henry Rich treated his mother-in-law as a stranger. In 1618 Pory championed the cause of an ancient servant of hers who was seeking admission to Sutton's Hospital, and he was in touch with her as late as 1632 when, in a letter of 17 March, he quoted her concerning her son-in-law, Lord Holland.

If the supposition that Pory lost Isabel to Sir Henry Rich is correct (thin though the basis for it be), his action late in 1618 is further evidence that he was able to forgive and forget, and that Carleton's advice to him had been sound and effective. It was in the late winter of that year that Pory reported that he was engaged by Robert Rich, father of Henry, in "some employment for the marchants."

∾ A LETTER ABOUT PARLIAMENT

[John Pory to Sir Ralph Winwood, 17 July 1610, The Duke of Buccleuch, Drumlanrig Castle, Thornhill, Dumfriesshire. Sir Ralph Winwood (1563?–1617) was English agent to the States-General of Holland from 1603 to 1614.]

Right honourable my very good lord
My letters dated yesterday being Monday the 16. of July, I supposed, should have bene delivered by Captain Conway;[110] but his journey being putt off till Thursday, my lady your best friend hath recommended them to this bearer. By whom (because this day in the success may proove either the happiest or the unhappiest parliament day since his Majesties coming in)[111] I cannot but advertise your lordship what hath passed. This morning my lord Treasurer,[112] who together with my lord Privy Seal,[113] my lord Chamberlain, & my lord of Worcester[114] went yester night to

110. Possibly the Captain Thomas Conway who, about 1618, was recorded as "adventuring" £37 10 in the Virginia Company.

111. On 17 July 1610 King James offered to accept £200,000 yearly in lieu of Tenures. This was the result of a conference held that afternoon between committees of both houses of Parliament. The king's written message came to be called "the Great Contract between king and people." Pory, of course, was a member of this parliament and undoubtedly witnessed the scene he describes here.

112. Robert Cecil, Earl of Salisbury (1563?–1612), was treasurer from 1608 to 1612. His father had held this post under Elizabeth, from 1572 to 1599.

113. Henry Howard, Earl of Northampton (1540–1614), was keeper of the privy seal from 1608 to 1614.

114. Edward Somerset, fourth Earl of Worcester (1553–1628).

Thebalds[115] to know his Majesties pleasure returned this answere to our 6. last demandes which we presented as additions to be putt into the bargain which we are now to make with his Majesty. To the first & second, (which were that in case of 1. outlawries[116] & 2. attaindours[117] the debte of the delinquent should first be payd before his Majesty should make any seisure) it was answered his Majesty was well pleased to graunt them. To the third and fourth, (namely 3. that it might be lawful to arrest the kings servante without leave; and 4. that no man should be inforced to lende mony to the king, nor to give a reason why he would not) his Majesty sent us an answere, that because we brought presidentes of antiquity to strengthen these demandes he allowed not of any presidents drawn from the times of usurping or decaying princes or of people too bold & wanton; that he desired not to governe in that commonwealth, where subjects should be assured of all thinges and hope for nothing, it was one thing submittere principatū legibus, and another thing submittere principatū subditis; that he would not leave to posterity such a mark of weaknes upon his reigne: and therfore his conclusion was: Non placet petitio: non placet exemplum: yet with this mittigation, that in Matters of lones he would refuse no reasonable excuse; nor should my lord Chamberlaine deny the arresting of any of his Majesties servantes if just cause were shewed. The fifte, 5. that in cases criminal the party accused might bring in witnesses to clear himselfe, was denyed by his Majesty; because it would be a manie occasion of perjury. For (said he) if Men will forswear themselves for an oxe or a Sheep, how much more for to save the life of a friend. That it was a matter of conscience, and therfore his Majesty could not part with it for mony. The 6.th his Majesty granted which was the repealing of a clause of a statute in 34.th of Hen. 8. wherby the King had power to make arbitrary lawes over the Welchmen: their loyalty, faith & obedience was well knowen, and he would not leave a marke of separation upon them in point of freedome. From hence my lord

115. Theobalds Park, seat of Robert Cecil, Earl of Salisbury, was acclaimed as the finest house in England. It was located two miles southwest of Cheshunt, Herts, and it was here that James I died.

116. Act or process of putting a man out of the protection of law, hence banishment or exile.

117. An attainder was the unalterable consequence of a judicial or a legislative sentence for treason or felony. It involved the forfeiture or escheat of all the real and personal property of the condemned person and such "corruption of blood" that he could neither receive nor transmit by inheritance, sue or testify in any court, or claim any legal protection or rights.

Tresurer came to the price, and here he said, that the King would no more rise and fall like a marchant; that he would not have a flower of his crowne (meaning the court of wards)[118] so much tossed, that it was too dainty to be so handled; and then he said he must deliver the very countenance and character of the kings minde out of his own handwriting. Which before he read, he said he would acquaint us with a pleasant conceipt of his Majesty as concerning the numbers: 9. skore M. pounds[119] which was our number he could not affect, because 9. was the number of the poets who were alwayes beggars though they served so many muses; and eleven was the number of the Apostles when the traytour Judas was away and therfore might best be affected by his Majesty, but there was a mean number which might accord us both & that was ten, which (said my lord Treš) is a sacred number; for so many were gods commandments which tend to vertue and edification. This his lordship read a very short letter directed from his Majesty to the lordes; some fragmentes wherof I remember to be these: It shall now (saith his Majesty) appeare, in whose hart sincerity is lodged, you may now be confident, saith hee, what to impart to your fellowes. I am loath to contract for all things. My cheef Strength I must derive from my subjects love, And because the lower house would reduce me to a more maiorum, we meane not to vary from that antient greatness of our predecessours. My demand for all together must be £200000. Hereupon my lord Treasurer inferred that the King being come lower by £20000 and that since he had granted sundry demands of importance never dreamt on, when he made his last stoupe from 14. skore to 11. skore thousand pounds that it would beseem us to meet with our soveraigne halfe way. And for my selfe (saith that noble lorde) no subject offers to his country as I have offered; for in thus relinquishing the court of Wardes, I am robbed of my right arme, and of the greatest strength I have to merit the love of many: And therfore although as Treasurer I have pressed very far for his Majesties advantage, yet as Master of the Wardes I have deserved no imputation: what should hinder us from so eminent a good? If poverty, it is but paupertas imaginari![120] Though we go not all uno gradu, yet lett us go una via if this be refused, inter peritura vivimus, &c.[121] And now for a close, to have

118. A court dealing with wardships or guardianships. Wardship carried with it the right to dispose of the ward in marriage and to retain the rents and profits of his land, subject only to the ward's right to suitable support.

119. A marginal note adds, "We offered 9. skore M. pounds. The king demanded eleven skore M. pounds."

120. "Fancied Poverty," Seneca, *Epistulae ad Lucilium* 20. 13.

121. We live amid perishable things.

all sowernes and all jelousies buried at our parting, I must crave excuse & pardon of you gentlemen of the lower house, if any of you have conceived any mistaking to proceed this session out of these lipps. And the like loving opinion I treasure up concerning the generality of your house and of every particular person therof. And so as we were departing he called us back againe, & told us that now he had delivered his Majesties final & peremptory resolution, that the distance was little & the bargain advantagious if we now refused, his Majesty would instantly dissolve the parlament & would never make the like offer to this assembly. So we all returned to the house, we instantly putt it to the question, and yielded to give his Majesty a perpetual revenue of £200000 a yeare; mary upon these conditions: First, that the court of Wardes be dissolved (together with the dependances, which are Respite of Homage, Restraint of Alienation, the Prefines and the Post fines pro lincentia concordandi)[122] Item that Purveiance be quite taken away & to that ende, that the ~~offices~~ autority [sic] of the greencloth be putt downe; Item that Informers be banished Item that his Majesty shall claime no old debts; Item that he shall lay claime to no lands which have bene 3. score yeares out of his possession. Item that contrary to the present use, all his Majesties patentes be strictly interpreted against the King & benighe for the Subject. Item that Lessees be not turned out of possession for nonpayment; Item that the subject may be permitted to plead a general plea against his Majesty, &ct And divers other particulars of great moment. Now remaines there to be resolved on the assurance, & with what cordes we shall binde Sampsons handes that is to say his Majesties prerogatives; and secondly the maner and means of levy, which will proove a busines of great intricacy, and these two branches are referred till the next session of parlament which will be in October at the farthest. And so for this time the King and Commons are like to part in the lovingest termes, that ever any subjects of England did rise from parlament. And here I must acquaint your lordship with a bill that is now passing in the higher house for his Majesties and the Princes[123] safety inflicting the most Exquisite torturs upon any that attempt his Majesties death, &ct What should I say more, that Sir Ferdinando Dudley heyre to the lord Dudley, was yesterday married to my lord Beauchamp's only daughter,[124] who hath £5000 in

122. In accordance with the freedom of agreeing.
123. Henry Frederick (1594–1612), Prince of Wales.
124. Sir Ferdinando Dudley married Honora, daughter of Edward Seymour, styled Lord Beauchamp.

present to her marriage, & shall have £5000 more. I do imagine I have perfectly tyred your lordship because I have wearied my selfe. Therfore here I will make a stand. To Sir Hatton Cheek[125] I humbly desire to be remembered. God have you in his holy protection.

Your lordships most humbly at commande

[Postscript] Sir W. Cope, my Lady & my Mistress are all in good health, & remember their affectionat love & service to your lordship.

∾ A LETTER ABOUT THE DEATH OF SIR WALTER RALEIGH

[John Pory to Sir Dudley Carleton, 31 October 1618, Public Record Office, State Papers, 14/103/61.]

Right honorable and my singular good lorde,
Albeit I make no doubte, but your lordship shall from diverse of your friends be advertised of the manner of Sir Walter Raleghs death; yet being a matter of so muche marke & renowne, it is fitt, that all tounges & pennes both good & bad shoulde be employed about it. This day Senenight therefore, as I was writing my last letter to your lordship Sir Walter Ralegh being sent for from the tower to come to the lordes at Whitehall, was there tolde by their lordships that it was his Majestyes pleasure he should dye upon the olde sentence,[126] and therfore willed him within three dayes to provide himselfe. His Majesties pleasure being resolutely so, Sir Walter became an humble suitour, that his Majesty would dispense with the ordinary punishment, and would permitte him to be beheaded.[127] On Wednesday he was by the headsman of the Tower brought to the kinges benche upon a writt of Scire facias.[128] There my lord Cheife Justice[129] having made a shorte speache, demanded of Sir Walter Ralegh what he could saye for himselfe, why he

125. Cheek and Pory were at Cambridge about the same time and may have known each other there. He subscribed to the second Virginia charter, 1609, and was killed in a duel by Sir Thomas Dalton in 1610.

126. In November 1603 Raleigh had been found guilty of conspiring against James I. He was reprieved the following month, however, but was confined with his wife and son in the Tower until 1616.

127. Beheading in England was the usual form of execution for offenders of high rank. It was practiced first in 1076 and last in 1747.

128. A judicial writ founded upon some matter of record and requiring the party proceeded against to show cause why the record should not be enforced, annulled, or vacated.

129. Sir Henry Montagu (1563?–1642) who was chief justice of the king's bench only from 1616 to 1620.

should not be executed upon the former sentence. His answere was, his Majesty had suffered him nowe to live 15. years since the pronouncing therof, and besides had given him a commission to be his lieutenant general over an army at sea, wherein he styled him, our beloved & trusty subjecte, &c gave him power of life and death; which his Majesty would never have done to the man he should esteeme a Traytour; Ergo this commission was equivalent to a Pardon. Mr Atturny[130] replyed that this without a speciall pardon would not serve his turne; and that if his Majesty had spared his life 15. yeares he was the more bounde to his clemency; might still have continued till his dying day, had not he since that time have committed some things, which had given his Majesty just cause of displeasure. Sir Walter Ralegh desired those things might be specified, and he would give satisfaction. No, said Mr Atturny, we must not enter into particulars. Then added my lord Chiefe Justice, that if Sir Walter had none other thing to alledge for himselfe, that the formere sentence must stand good, and that the lieutenant by vertue of a writte ought to deliver him to the Sheriffs of Middlesex. At the stayer foot coming downe from the kinges benche stood the clerke of the Crowne with the same writte directed to the lieutenant to deliver him, and another to the Sheriff to receive him, and to carry him thence to the Gatehouse, and the next morning from the gatehouse to the place of his beheading, which was the Parliament yarde. On Thursday morning therfore being my lord Mayours feast-day, before eight of the clock the sheriffs brought him upon the Scaffolde. Spectators there were besides knights & gentlemen of good quality, the Earle of Arondell,[131] the Earle of Oxforde,[132] the Earle of Nothampton,[133] my lord of Doncaster,[134] my lord Sheffeilde,[135] my lord Percy,[136] & some others. The first

130. Sir Henry Yelverton (1566–1629).
131. Thomas Howard, Earl of Arundel (1586–1646), privy councillor.
132. Henry De Vere, eighteenth Earl of Oxford (1593–1625).
133. Spencer Compton, second Earl of Northampton (1601–43).
134. James Hay, first Earl of Carlisle, first Viscount Doncaster, and first Baron Hay (d. 1636).
135. Sir Edmund Sheffield (1564?–1646), president of the north and Lord Lieutenant of Yorkshire, 1603–19. He was a member of the councils of both the Virginia and New England Companies.
136. Henry Percy, ninth Earl of Northumberland (1564–1632). He was a prisoner in the Tower at this time "for contempt and misprison of treason" in connection with the gunpowder plot. While in the Tower he saw something of his fellow prisoner, Raleigh, and employed the scientist and Roanoke explorer Thomas Hariot, among others, to assist him in his studies. A comment in Pory's letter of 10 November 1632 at the death of Northumberland calling the Earl his "noble Patrone," suggests that Pory was also one of them. See also fn. 10 to the letter of 7 November 1618.

words he uttered were, I give god thankes, I am come to dye in the light, and not in the darknes. Then because his voice was but weake, he besought their lordships to come out of Sir Randal Crewes[137] windowe where they stood, and to mount upon the Scaffolde, which they did. Then he asked my lord of Arondel whither he had not kept touche with him, in not turning Pirate when he was abroad, and in coming home notwithstanding his ill success? His lordship answered: yes. Then he cleared my lord Carewe[138] & my lord of Doncaster from ever persuading him to goe serve the French kinge or from being acquainted with any suche busines, as Stukley[139] had accused them, and besides, that he never tolde Stukely any suche thinge. He then denyed that ever he spoke to Mannering[140] Sir Lewys Stukelies French Apothecary, any disloyal or dishonourable worde concerning the kinge, which seems to have bene the chief incentive of his death. He said farther that he never sawe any commission, letter, nor seale from the Frenche king. He had a desire indeed to have gone into France, to have saved his life & liberty & to have renewed his voyage. But he had never any plott with the Frenche king or his Agent. He confessed he blistered himselfe at Sir Edward Parhams[141] and that it was a faulte & a weaknes, but for the saveguarde of his life; and this he had [learned?] from a wiser man then himselfe, even Daniel the lordes annointed, whoe for the same ende [founde?] himselfe mad. He protested, that although he were of the Contrary faction to my lord of Essex,[142] and had helped to plucke him downe, yet never had he a hande in his bloud, that is to saye, he was none of them that procured his death; nor (as he had long time bene accused) did he rejoice or smyle at it. Hee besides affirmed that his voyage was upon no fained projecte, but that there is a true golde-mine within three miles of Saint Tomé, the towne which his people burnte. All these & diverse other thinges (which in my next I will write) he affirmed upon his salvation, as a man that had but halfe an hower to live, by which time he was confident, his soule should peirce the

137. Sir Ranulphe, Radolph, or Randolph Crewe (1558–1646), of Cheshire. He was a barister and former speaker of the House of Commons.

138. George Carew, Baron Carew of Clopton (1555–1629).

139. Sir Lewis Stucley or Stukely (d. 1620), vice-admiral of Devonshire. He was appointed keeper of Raleigh on his return from the Orinoco. In this capacity his supposed unfair conduct made him intensely unpopular.

140. Mannourie, Stukely's physician, was described by John Chamberlain as "the runagatt French phisician."

141. Sir Edward Parham, of Lincoln, had been knighted by James on 23 July 1603 in the Royal Garden at Whitehall just before James's coronation.

142. Robert Devereux, second Earl of Essex (1566–1601).

the cloudes, and that nowe he was not to flatter even kinges, nor to feare any mortall man, and now to lye he said or to dissemble, was to affront the heavens, & to skorne the deity. Then the Deane of Westminster[143] asked him in what faith or religion he meant to day [die]; he said in the faith professed by the Churche of Englande, and that he hoped to be saved, & to have his Sinnes washed away by the pretious bloud and Merits of our Saviour Christ. Then, before he shoulde say his prayers, because the morning was sharpe, the sheriff offered him to bring him downe off the scaffolde to warme him by a fire. No, good Mr Sheriff (said he) lett us dispatche; for within this quarter of this hower mine ague will come upon me, and if I be not dead before then mine enemies will saye that I quake for feare. So he made a most divine & admirable prayer, and then he rose up, clapped his handes & saide, Nowe I am going to god. He then bid the hangman shewe him his axe, which having poized in his hand, he felte upon the edge, saying, here is a medicin will cure me of all my diseases, and so delivered it the hangman againe. Then he putt off his gowne, untrussed himselfe, and put off his band & doublett, and most gracefully took his leave at all 4. sides of the Scaffolde. Laying his head downe the block, he was angry with the hangman that would have blindfolded his eyes, saying you thinke I feare the shadowe of the axe, when I fear not the axe itself. And so when he should holde up his handes saying his last prayer he bad him strike. Many other circumstances, and pointes of substance there were bothe before and at the time of his execution, which were very memorable; but nowe mine other occasions will not suffer me to recount all. The rest I must of force leave till the next Satturday. Meane while & ever wishing your lordship and my most honoured lady all imaginable felicity, I reste

Your lordships ever most humbly at your service

[Postscript] This night the king is said to be come to Whitehall. The Queene at Hampton court is prettily recovered of her sickness, she eates her meat & sleeps well, onely hath some debility in her feet. Mr Richard Martin[144] the newe Recorder lyes a dying. Our East India Company have contracted with the king of Persia to bring all the silkes of that Empire by way of the Persian Gulfe, paying one third in mony, & the other two thirdes in comodity. So

143. Dr. Robert Tounson, who later became the Bishop of Salisbury.
144. Richard Martin (1570–1618) died on 3 November, according to Pory's letter of the 7th. John Chamberlain, however, writing on the same date as Pory, noted that Martin died on Sunday, the 1st.

shall they undoe the Turke bring that for £150000 by the yeare, which costeth Christendome £800000. and unspeakably inriche our kingdome, themselves at leaste.

[Marginal note] Every man that sawe Sir Walter Ralegh dye sayd it was impossible for any man to shewe more Decorum, courage, or piety; and that his death will doe more hurte to the faction that sought it, then ever his life could have done.

2. In Virginia ~~

Late in October 1618 George Yeardley, a man of considerable military experience and formerly acting governor of Virginia, was "chosen governour of Virginia . . . in my lord de la Wares [Sir Thomas West's] place (who dyed in Canada)." Yeardley's plans, Pory wrote on 25 October, were to go "instantly thither with some twoe ships and about 300 men & boys, the greatest difficulties of that plantation, they begin now to enjoye both commodity & wealth." More than a month later Yeardley was still in London making necessary arrangements for the Virginia voyage, yet several ships stood ready to sail at his command. "To grace him the more," John Chamberlain commented on 28 November, "the King knighted him this weeke at Newmarket; which hath set him up so high that he flaunts it up and downe the streets in extraordinarie braverie, with fourteen or fifteen fayre liveries after him."[1] Five days later Chamberlain further reported that "the greatest newes I have is that Master Pory is in the way of high preferment, for yesterday [2 December 1618] he was chosen Secretarie of Virginia for three yeares, and is upon his departure thether the end of this weeke with the new governor Sir George Yardly, who married his cousen germain as he tells me: no question but he will become there a sufficient sober man seeing there is no wine in all that climat."[2]

Pory, of course, had known of the possibility of such an appointment before it became official and on 28 November had written to his confidant, Sir Dudley Carleton, some of the details. On the previous day he had been chosen to be secretary in Virginia by the Council of the Virginia Company composed of Henry Wriothesley, Earl of Southampton; Sir Robert Rich, soon to become the second Earl of Warwick; Edmund Lord Sheffield; and William Lord Paget. Sir George Yeardley, the newly designated governor of the colony whose wife, Temperance Flowerdew, was Pory's first cousin, "infinitly desires my company," Pory wrote, and

---

1. Chamberlain to Carleton, 28 November 1618. Norman E. McClure, ed., *The Letters of John Chamberlain* (Philadelphia, 1939), 2:188.
2. Chamberlain to Carleton, 3 December 1618. Ibid., 2:190.

had asked for the appointment himself without Pory's seeking the position.

The secretary-designate was anxious to know what allowances he might expect to enable him to prepare for the Atlantic voyage as well as what maintenance he would receive in the colony, but his questions revealed the council members to be "as dry as Pumystones." Passage would be expensive and living in Virginia might also, so Pory decided "not to adventure my Carkase in so dangerous a busines for nothing." Yeardley ventured to say that the position would be worth at least £200 a year, and he offered to advance Pory £50 "to sett me forthe." With this assurance he was seriously considering the offer, and he was to accept or decline not later than the following night. In the event he refused it, Pory kept his options open by intimating that he would be most happy to enter Carleton's service "in case I do not embrace this." The time allowed him to reach a decision was short, but it was adequate. The possibility of substantial financial reward existed, and the prestige of the position appealed to Pory's vanity. He accepted promptly.

Secretary of Virginia

Yeardley's commission as governor was issued on 18 November,[3] and Pory received his as secretary shortly afterwards. Previous secretaries in Virginia (Gabriel Archer, Mathew Scriviner, William Strachey, Ralph Hamor, and John Rolfe) had had informal appointments; Pory, whose title was to be Secretary of Estate, was the first to receive a commission from the Virginia Company.[4] Although Yeardley, Pory, and others accompanying them were ready to sail now, they actually did not depart England until 19 January 1619. After three months at sea they reached Jamestown on 18 April, and Pory was soon thereafter made a member of the council for the government of the colony.[5]

Nearly four years later charges were trumped up accusing Pory of causing the delay of the sailing date by about two months and attempting to show that he had divided his allegiance between the governor of Virginia and other officials of the Virginia Com-

3. William G. Stanard and Mary Newton, *The Colonial Virginia Register* (Albany, N.Y., 1902), p. 14.
4. Junius R. Fishburne, Jr., "The Office of Secretary of State in Virginia" (Ph.D. diss., Tulane University, 1971), p. 47, and passim.
5. Alexander Brown, *The Genesis of the United States* (Boston, 1890), 2:970.

pany on one hand and the faction within the company that has been blamed for much of the internal dissension in the Virginia Company on the other. This accusation against Pory was repeated without question by many of the early historians of Virginia, among whom William Stith is most noteworthy.[6] Before accepting the charges as true, however, one should investigate the facts of the case. Officials of the Virginia Company were desperately trying to ward off attacks from all sides; they were accused of neglecting the colony in Virginia and as a result were about to lose their charter and the privileges which it granted. Pory later was one of the members of a royal committee appointed to investigate conditions in Virginia and report to the Privy Council on the state of affairs there, hence he was liable to attack from within the company for all his past actions.[7] The charges against Pory were never mentioned at the time they were alleged to have occurred but were first presented more than three years later.

Governor Yeardley's initial duty after arriving in Virginia was to try his predecessor in the office, Deputy Governor Samuel Argall, on several charges. Argall was accused of excessive greed for his personal benefit whenever opportunities presented themselves. Pory himself, a few months later, accused Argall of having fitted out a ship to raid Spanish vessels plying their trade to the New World "more for love of gaine the root of all evill, then for any true love he bore to this Plantation."[8]

The specific charges against Pory were that he caused a delay in sailing long enough to send a warning to Argall of pending events and thus enable him to escape punishment. But the vagueness of the accusation is important: "Sir George Yeardley by the perswasions (as is vehemently to be presumed of Mr. Pory whom the said Earle [of Warwick] had lately comended unto Sir Thomas Smith then Treasuror for the Secretaries place of Virginia) [was] spending much time unnecesarily uppon our English Coaste," the company charged on 7 May 1623. It actually was Sir Robert Rich who sent word to his friend Argall, but Rich had been one of those who recommended Pory as a suitable man to be secretary.

Other explanations for the delay in sailing can also be found. On the night of 18 November 1618, just after Yeardley had been given his commission, a flaming comet appeared, and this was

6. William Stith, *The History of the First Discovery and Settlement of Virginia* (London, 1753), p. 157.
7. Richard L. Morton, *Colonial Virginia* (Chapel Hill, N.C., 1960), 1:55.
8. Pory to Carleton, 30 September 1619.

generally regarded as a bad omen for the new governor and his party. Pory's letter of 28 November to Carleton recited some of the dire forecasts. The comet remained visible until after Christmas, and superstition prevented the sailing of the Virginia expedition until it had safely disappeared.[9]

The weather at that season of the year, in the middle of winter, also played a practical part in determining the sailing date. Yeardley had been in Virginia before, and in past military service abroad he had had more experience at sea than Pory. It is unrealistic to imagine that on a mere pretense Pory could so influence either Yeardley or the captain of the ship as to delay the sailing by so much as a day.

An explanation of Argall's warning may be found in John Smith's statement that "it is neere as much trouble, but more danger, to sail from London to Plymouth than from Plymouth to New England, so that half the voyage would be saved," he said, by sailing from Plymouth instead of London.[10] The warning to Argall actually was dispatched from London to Plymouth by Lord Rich and from Plymouth on an early ship to Jamestown.[11]

Events in Jamestown were recorded by John Rolfe in Smith's *Generall Historie*. "For to begin with the yeere of our Lord, 1619," he wrote, "there arrived a little Pinnace privately from England about Easter [28 March 1619] for Captaine Argall, who taking order for his affaires, within foure or five daies returned in her, and left for his Deputy, Captaine Nathaniel Powell. On the eighteenth of Aprill, which was but ten or twelve daies after, arrived Sir George Yeardley."[12]

Even Yeardley did not escape the suspicions of those who were eager to blame someone on the other side for warning Argall. The arrest of his predecessor would certainly have been an unpleasant duty, and there must have been a friendship between the two men. About two years later Yeardley's first son was given the

9. "A Declaracon made by the Counsell for Virginia and Principall Assistants for the Sumer Ilandes of their Judgments Touchinge one Originall Great Cause of the Dissentions in the Companies and Present Opposicons," in Susan M. Kingsbury, *The Records of the Virginia Company of London* (Washington, 1906–35), 2:404. Stillman Drake and C. D. O'Malley, trans., *The Controversy on the Comets of 1618* (Philadelphia, 1960) contains contemporary reports including Galileo's observations, on three comets that appeared in 1618.

10. *Collections of the Massachusetts Historical Society*, 9:18–19.

11. Kingsbury, *Records of the Virginia Company*, 2:403.

12. Lyon G. Tyler, *Narratives of Early Virginia, 1606–1625* (New York, 1907), p. 335.

baptismal name of Argall.[13] Quite early Pory saw signs of Yeardley's regard for Argall. He spoke of Yeardley's "more then ordinary affection towards Captain Argall."[14] Although Yeardley felt that Argall "hath in him to deserve much" he did "wishe that Captain Argall being riche, a Bachelour, and devoid of charge, would not so excessivly intende his owne thrifte."[15]

Pory's early fears about not receiving suitable recompense for adventuring his "carkase in so dangerous a business" as the secretaryship for Virginia seem to have been warranted. Some six months after his arrival he learned that he would have to maintain himself on whatever fees he could collect. Yeardley, he said, anticipated that fees for the position would amount to £300 sterling, but 50 of these, Pory noted, were due the governor for the amount advanced to enable him to prepare for the voyage to Virginia. After all debts were paid, "I pray God the remainder may amounte to a hundred more. As yet I have gotten nothing," he wrote Carleton on 30 September 1619. At the end of the year he still had "received not a farthing."[16]

Pory reminded Carleton that his fees had been set by "a warrant from the Governor: and Counsell . . . according as it was there ordered in courte before my coming awaye." However, "if the Company shalbe pleased to confirme unto me that, which all men of reason here do thinke to be but reasonable, I shall esteem both my hazard and my paines well bestwoed, although, do what I can, I feare me, that at my three yeares end I shall skarce make a saving voiage."[17]

Pory, much to his regret, learned soon enough that the company in London had abolished the fees by which his office was supported.[18] At a general quarter court held on 17 May 1620, it was "agreed and confirmed . . . that Mr. Porye, the secretary, and his successors in that place, should have 500 acres of land belonging to that office and twenty tenants to be planted thereupon, whereof ten to be sent this year and ten the next, and the Secretary there from henceforward should receive no fees for himself, and the fees

13. J. H. R. Yardley, *Before the Mayflower* (London, 1931), pp. 217–18. Brown, *Genesis of the United States*, 2:1065.

14. Pory to Sir Edwin Sandys, 13 Jan. 1620.

15. Ibid.

16. Ibid.

17. Ibid.

18. *Collections of the Massachusetts Historical Society*, 9:16.

to be paid his clerk for writing and other charges to be rated there by the court."[19]

At the court held on 26 June it was reported that a charter was then being prepared for several officers in Virginia, including Pory, "to be confirmed in the nexte Courte if itt be approved."[20] From henceforth, it was decided, the "Companie here shall not be charged with the maintenance of the officers there: But they shallbe maintained there, out of the publique Lands."[21]

The governor and the secretary of Virginia, even though related by marriage, seem not always to have been on the best of terms insofar as official duties were concerned. Governor Yeardley was suspicious of Pory's loyalties, having been warned in advance by Sir Edwin Sandys to keep a close watch over him. This the governor did, and he wrote Sandys sometime in 1619, "By experience I have found your Judgment not deceaved." Nevertheless, Pory was essential to his administration, and as Yeardley bluntly expressed it, "nessitty [sic] hath no law and better a bad foole then none or worse." In a letter of 20 July Yeardley mentioned having "entercepted" two letters written by Pory to his old friend, Robert Rich, Earl of Warwick. The governor wrote, "You may please to judg of in your wisdome what concernes the Publike, for anything that shall tende to my private damage I forgive both him and them, and leave it to the Lorde."[22]

Having suspected Pory of corresponding with the faction within the management of the company to which he was opposed, Yeardley supervised Pory's work closely.[23] "Without his commandement I did nothing," Pory remarked, "and that which I did, he viewed and reviewed still to a syllable . . . and he constantly avowes and Justifies every iota and title."[24] Pory knew that his letters to the Earl of Warwick had been seen by the governor, but

19. Robert A. Brock, "Abstract of the Proceedings of the Virginia Company of London, 1619–1624," in *Collections of the Virginia Historical Society*, n.s. (Richmond, Va., 1888–89), 1:64.

20. Kingsbury, *Records of the Virginia Company*, 1:375.

21. Peter Force, *Tracts and Other Papers, Relating Principally to the Origin, Settlement and Progress of the Colonies in North America from the Discovery of the Country to the Year 1776* (Washington, 1884), vol. 3, Tract No. 5.

22. Yeardley to [?], 20 July 1619, in Kingsbury, *Records of the Virginia Company*, 3:152; Yeardley to [Sandys?], [1619], ibid., 3:125–26.

23. For an account of the factions within the company see Wesley Frank Craven, *Dissolution of the Virginia Company* (New York, 1932). Pory actually corresponded with Rich and with Sandys, who were representatives of both factions and were old acquaintances, but it was his communications with Rich that got him into more trouble.

24. Pory to Sandys, 13 January 1620.

"his lordship I knowe (so noble is he) will not be implacable." Pory was convinced that outsiders were trying to drive a wedge between the governor and himself. "The imbecillity of some of Sir George his freinds, who not havinge courage enough to defende his letter by the fflemish man of warr, layd all the envy upon me, as if Sir George had bene so weake, as to have signed to any thinge ignorantly, or against his will or as if I had counterfaycted his hand and seale. My comfort is that this wronge hath advanced me to so high a dignity as it is nowe in my power to pardon my betters."[25]

In his own defense in this matter of questioned loyalty, Pory presented a very eloquent case. To Sir Edwin Sandys, treasurer of the Virginia Company, he wrote,

> Whatsoever errours of mine be represented back hither (for in the distemper I was in, I could not chuse, but committe some) I shall be more willing to amende, then ever I was to committe, and shall honour them most, that read me my lesson most roundly. And whosoever do so, shall in my conceipte do far better, then those others (who they were, I knowe not) that by the Marigolde putt this governour for the time (whenas I served him with the greatest fidelity and zeale that was possible) into so many violent nedles Jealousies against me, which notwithstanding had not the force to batter downe my patience of prooff. . . . And you shall perceive, howe I have concurred with you to close up the breache, which was in danger to have growen wider. So have I ever since my coming hither performed the part of a true friend, and that for the publique good, wherein I pray god, we may all have Joye.[26]

Both Rich and Sandys (with whom Pory had served in Parliament) were old friends, and Pory tried to treat both alike: "That lawe of justice and friendship so to doe right to one friend, as to beware of offring wrong to another, I have as duely observed as I could any way devise," was the way he expressed it in his letter of 12 June 1620 to Sandys.

Official Duties

Most of Pory's official duties as secretary kept him at Jamestown, but occasionally he was required to visit other settlements. On 14 December 1619, for example, he drew up a certificate at Charles City showing the arrival of the ship *Margaret* and listing

25. Pory to Sandys, 12 June 1620.
26. Ibid.

the names of thirty-five new settlers. A similar certificate was dated from "Barklay" plantation on 29 January 1621.[27]

Pory, as secretary, had a clerk to handle some of the lesser details of the office, including actual writing, but he himself undoubtedly served as a public letter writer. He once mentioned having received little thanks from "the most of those I doe service for."[28] He certainly made copies of the letters drawn up by the governor, frequently adding his own signature as secretary after the governor's signature, and sometimes also adding a postscript of his own.[29]

There is a strong possibility that Pory was the author of the publication, *A Note of the Shipping, Men and Provisions Sent for Virginia in the Yeere 1619* published in London each of the three years during which he was secretary, 1619 through 1621.[30] It may have been to the first of these that John Chamberlain referred on 28 June 1620 when he wrote Sir Dudley Carleton, "I have sent you Master Pories relation as you willed me, and a little pamflet newly come out of the same subject."[31]

The oldest land patent still on file in the Virginia Land Office is one dated 20 February 1619 [1620], signed by George Yeardley as governor and by Pory as secretary. The original of this grant has been lost, but an official copy made in 1683 is preserved among the public records.[32]

Unofficial Duties

Aside from his strictly official duties as secretary, Pory found time to see Virginia and to write praises of the new country he visited. His careful and detailed observations at this early period are interesting for both what he reported and the hope and faith he had in the country.

By way of illustrating Pory's varied interests and activities while serving in Virginia, his participation in the efforts to establish an iron mine may be cited. The company had sent two Germans

27. Kingsbury, *Records of the Virginia Company*, 3:230, 426–27.
28. Pory to Sandys, 13 January 1620.
29. Kingsbury, *Records of the Virginia Company*, 3:451 and passim.
30. A. W. Pollard and G. R. Redgrave, *A Short-title Catalogue of Books Printed in England, Scotland, and Ireland . . . 1475–1640* (London, 1950), nos. 24842, 24842a, and 24843.
31. McClure, *Letters of John Chamberlain*, 2:309.
32. Nell Marion Nugent, *Cavaliers and Pioneers, Abstracts of Virginia Land Patents and Grants, 1623–1800* (Richmond, Va., 1934), 1:xxiv, 109.

who were "skillfull in mynes" to open the industry in the vicinity of Jamestown, but after seeing their attempts to find ore, Pory sought the aid of a friend whom he considered to be as skillfull as they. Setting out together, expecting "to finde better Comodity, and of lesse labor," Pory and his friend took samples from areas which the Germans had not examined. Pory concluded that "some skillfull men should have perused the country for a whole yeare . . . and should have bene sure of some abundant Iron mine and fit places to worke it in."[33]

Secretary Pory, having traveled widely before coming to Virginia, proved to be a careful observer. His experience was invaluable in the new colony, and his comments on the potentials of the country are interesting. His practical advice on several immediate problems was accepted and found to be correct.

Salt was a very important item of commerce, and it was essential for the survival of the colony. Pory found Virginians "boyling sea water into salt in kettles," a process which he called "toylesome and erroneous." He offered to "undertake in one day to make as much salt by the heate of the sunne, after the manner used in ffrance, Spaine, and Italy, as can be made in a yeare" by the colonists' method. Pory probably did know something about salt making, a process he surely had observed in his travels. The town of Bridgwater, which he had represented in Parliament, was one of the seventeenth-century centers of salt refining in southwestern England, and he may also have seen the process there. To improve methods in the colony, however, Pory suggested to an official of the Virginia Company that they send over "men skillful in salt pondes, such as you may easily procure from Rochell, and if you can have none there, yet will some be found at Lymington, and in many other places in England."[34] This advice was accepted, and by May 1622 a "Rocheller" had arrived and selected suitable places for saltworks in Virginia, and work was getting underway.[35]

The possibilities of forest products—lumber as well as tar and pitch—did not seem promising to Pory. "ffor tymber and bourdes well may they serve for the use of the Colony," he said, "but in sendinge for the same expressly out of England, the fraight would cost double the price of the commodity." "ffor Pitch and

33. Pory to Sandys, 12 June 1620.
34. Ibid.
35. "A Note of the Shipping, Men and Provisions Sent and Provided for Virginia, . . . in the Yeere 1621," in Kingsbury, *Records of the Virginia Company*, 3:641.

tarre, true it is, that as some quantety hath heretofore bene made, so may there be some made hereafter, but some here that have lived longe in Poland doe say, that the worth will no way contravaile the chardge." The sparseness of the pine trees in Virginia, which would necessitate a large labor force, would make the lumber too expensive to produce, Pory thought.[36]

Of "Cordage," he predicted, "if our Virginia hempe and flaxe (which are sayd to be the most growinge thinges in the country) doe prosper, will the best in the world be made here, the stuffe by reporte being thrise as stronge as ours, and a greate deale more free from rottinge, and wearinge."

Silk he considered "a marvellous hopefull comodity in this Country, here beinge as many mulbery trees as in Persia, or in any other parte of the world besides."

For vineyards and grapes Pory expressed a great deal of interest and also in a "Mr Chanterton," whom he suspected of being an international spy operating under the guise of an authority on grapes and wine.

As secretary he let no opportunity pass by which he might send news of Virginia to his friends in England, and he even sent one letter by way of Canada. "This [letter]," he wrote Sir Edwin Sandys on 12 June 1620, "I thought expedyent to adde by the Duty nowe bound to trade and fish in Canada, where wee hope they will finde some men of Plymouth, to the ende that as you had wrytten by every one, so wee might ymitate your example." Strangely enough, it was this letter sent by Canada which contained advice to officers of the company in England on the shortest and best route to be followed in plotting a course for Virginia.[37]

Pory's hopes for the future must have sounded visionary indeed to those who understood the true state of affairs in Virginia when he arrived. In "A Briefe Declaration of the Planters of Virginia During the First Twelve Yeares when Sir Thomas Smyth was Governor of the Companie, and downe to this Present Tyme: by the Ancient Planters nowe remaininge Alive in Virginia," a pathetic scene was drawn. In April when Sir George Yeardley arrived, "James Citty" was made up of "only those houses that Sir Thomas Gates built in the tyme of his government, with one wherein the Governor allwayes dwelt, and a church, built wholly at the charge of the inhabitants of that citye, of timber, being fifty foote in length and twenty foot in breadth." At Henrico the ancient planters said

36. Pory to Sandys, 12 June 1620.
37. Ibid.

that they were no more than "three old houses, a poor ruinated Church, with some Few poore buildings in the Islande."[38]

From the moment of Yeardley's arrival, however, a renewed spirit began to appear. The new governor brought with him "Commissions and instructions from the Company for the better establishinge of a Commonwealth heere." By proclamation he let the people know "that those cruell lawes, by which we had soe longe been governed, were now abrogated, and that we were to be governed by those free lawes, which his Majesties subjects live under in Englande."[39] The charter of 1606, under which Virginia was first settled, had guaranteed that all people "within any of the limits and precincts of the said several colonies and plantations" regardless of age, sex, or race, should "have and enjoy all liberties, franchises, and immunities, within any of our other dominions, to all intents and purposes, as if they had been abiding and born, within this our realm of England, or any other of our said dominions."[40]

First Legislative Assembly

In order "that they might have a hand in the governinge of themselves," the ancient planters said, when Sir George Yeardley arrived "it was graunted that a generall Assemblie should be held yearly once, whereat were to be present the Governor and Counsell with two Burgesses from each Plantation, freely to be elected by the Inhabitantes thereof, this Assemblie to have power to make and ordaine whatsoever lawes and orders should by them be thought good and proffitable for our subsistance."[41]

This move toward more popular government in the colony was largely due to the efforts of Sir Edwin Sandys. His instructions reflected only one phase of a broad program of reform within the Virginia Company. More suitable colonists were seen as necessary for the well-being of the settlement in Virginia. Wider interests in

38. George Bancroft, "Introductory Note to Proceedings of the First Assembly of Virginia, 1619," in *Collections of the New-York Historical Society*, 2d sers., vol. 3, pt. 1, (New York, 1857):331.

39. Ibid.

40. W. W. Hening, ed. *The Statutes at Large, Being a Collection of all the Laws of Virginia, From the First Session of the Legislature in the Year 1619* (New York, 1823), 1:64. These same rights of Englishmen had been guaranteed in Sir Humphrey Gilbert's charter of 1578 and in the subsequent charters to Sir Walter Raleigh.

41. Bancroft, "Introductory Note," p. 332.

Conjectural painting of the 1619 assembly in session.

Conjectural sketch of the church at Jamestown in which the 1619 assembly met.

agriculture, a system of schools, inns for newcomers, and better homes for all the settlers were also essential. Martial law of the immediate past was abandoned and English common law instituted. The establishment of a legislature for the colony was also a part of the program, and instructions for its organization were included in the plans sent over with Governor Yeardley.

On 25 June 1619, the ship *Triall* arrived in Virginia with corn and cattle to relieve the people of their immediate fear of famine. Almost immediately afterwards the "governour and councell caused Burgesses to be chosen in all places."[42] It was directed that Burgesses to represent the people in an assembly were to be "elected by the People in their several Plantations,"[43] but exactly how the election was to be conducted was not specified. It is likely, however, that the whole male population except apprentices under age assembled and made their selections viva voce or by a show of hands. Such a method was followed in 1624 when representatives were chosen by "pluralitie of voyces."[44]

42. John Smith, *The Generall Historie of Virginia* (London, 1624), p. 126.
43. Robert Beverley, *The History of Virginia* (London, 1722), p. 35.
44. Kingsbury, *Records of the Virginia Company*, 4:449.

This was the first representative legislative body in America, and it was composed of the four members of the "Counsell of Estate": the Reverend Samuel Macocke, John Pory, Nathaniel Powell, and John Rolfe; and of twenty-two burgesses, two from each of the eleven settlements: James Citty, Charles Citty, the Citty of Henricus, Kiccowtan, Martin Brandon (Captain John Martin's plantation), Smyth's Hundred, Martin's Hundred, Argall's Gift, Flowerdieu Hundred, Captain Christopher Lawne's plantation, and Captain John Warde's plantation.

This new agency of government in Virginia was intended to be "a local reproduction, with appropriate modifications, of the English Constitutional system." The governor stood in approximately the same relationship to the Virginia Company that the ministers of the government in England stood to the crown, while the General Assembly stood in somewhat the same position as Parliament.[45] The assembly, it has been pointed out, was modeled on the old English county court and had powers that were both legislative and "to some extent judicial." The acts of the assembly, however, were not to become final and official until confirmed by the Virginia Company. On the other hand, enactments of the company for the colony were to be valid only upon approval of the assembly.[46]

On Friday, 30 July 1619, "more than a year before the Mayflower, with the Pilgrims, left the harbor of Southampton, and while Virginia was still the only British Colony on the whole continent of America,"[47] the elected representatives of the people gathered in the "Quire of the Churche"[48] at Jamestown to make laws governing themselves.

Speaker of the Assembly

The men settled down to work with very little formality. Pory, in the journal of the assembly that he kept, wrote that "the Governor, being sett downe in his accustomed place, those of the Counsel of Estate sate next him on both hands excepte onely the

45. Arthur D. Innes, *The Maritime and Colonial Expansion of England Under the Stuarts (1603–1714)* (London, 1932), p. 103.

46. John Fiske, *Old Virginia and Her Neighbors* (Boston, 1900), 1:178–79.

47. Bancroft, "Introductory Note," p. 334.

48. A new church had been built during Argall's governorship (1617–19), "wholly at the charge of the inhabitants of that cittie, of timber, being fifty foote in length and twenty foot in breadth" (Brown, *Genesis of the United States*, 2:835).

Secretary [that is, Pory, himself] then appointed Speaker, who sate right before him John Twine, clerke of the General assembly, being placed next the Speaker, and Thomas Pierse, the Sergeant, standing at the barre, to be ready for any service the Assembly shoulde comaund him."

The burgesses then took seats in the choir of the church while the Reverend Richard Bucke, an Oxford graduate, prayed "that it would please God to guide and sanctifie all our proceedings to his owne glory and the good of this plantation." All the burgesses were then "intreatted to retyre themselves into the body of the Churche, which being done, before they were fully admitted, they were called in order and by name, and so every man (none staggering at it) tooke the oathe of Supremacy, and entred the Assembly." Pory voiced an objection when the name of Captain John Warde was read because he had settled in Virginia without authority or commission from the Virginia Company or its officials. Warde was commanded to absent himself and "after much debate" the assembly agreed to readmit him, "because the Comission for authorising the General Assembly admitteth of two Burgesses out of every plantation without restrainte or exception."

After the case of Captain Warde had been settled, the governor suggested an examination of the burgesses representing Martin's Brandon, the plantation of Captain John Martin. A clause in the patent granted Martin by the company would not only "exempte him from that equality and uniformity of lawes and orders which the great charter saith are to extende over the whole Colony, but also from diverse such lawes as we must be enforced to make in the General Assembly." The whole assembly considered this case, and after calling Captain Martin himself for questioning and failing to get him to renounce the special grant of exemption from the laws of the colony, the burgesses from his plantation were denied seats in the assembly. Furthermore the other burgesses directed Pory, as Speaker, to "humbly demaunde of the Treasurer, Counsell and Company an exposition of this one clause . . . where it is saide That he is to enjoye his landes in as lardge and ample manner, to all intents and purposes, as any lord of any manours in England."[49]

49. This seems to anticipate the "Bishop of Durham" clause in the Carolana charter of 1629 granted to Sir Robert Heath and in subsequent charters. For an explanation of this later clause see Mattie Erma Edwards Parker, *North Carolina Charters and Constitutions (1578–1698)* (Raleigh, N.C., 1963), pp. xix, 62, 75, and passim. For an account of Martin's role in Virginia at this time and a possible connection between his actions and the dissolution of the Virginia Company a few years later see Richard Beale Davis, *George Sandys, Poet-Adventurer* (London, 1955), pp. 173–75.

This right to determine the qualification of its own membership was a perfectly logical right of a legislative body. In 1586 the House of Commons had asserted exclusive right to settle election disputes and to determine who was and was not a duly elected and qualified member.[50]

Numerous English customs, institutions, and other aspects of culture have been transplanted to America, but there are very few instances when one can point to a special place and time, and with any degree of certainty say that then and there a particular English practice was established in America. The introduction of the representative legislature at Jamestown on 30 July 1619, is one of those rare instances. Pory's parliamentary experience qualified him to do this. Just as it was on the banks of the Thames, so it was on the banks of the James. Business was conducted in a very orderly manner, and the procedure of the statement of a bill or matter to be discussed, followed by debate and final action, was quite like that followed in the House of Commons between 1605 and 1611 when Pory had been there.[51]

Organization of the Assembly

Having settled the matter of membership, Pory directed the General Assembly toward the real purpose for which it had been called. He recorded that he next "delivered in briefe to the whole assembly the occasions of their meeting," after which he "read unto them the commission for establishing the Counsell of Estate and the general Assembly, wherein their duties were described to the life." He then referred the various charters, commissions, and laws of the colony to two committees, which he probably appointed himself. The committees were to familiarize themselves with the provisions of these documents. Such a committee system began to evolve in the British House of Commons about 1604, and by 1610, before Pory left Parliament, standing committees had developed which met frequently or even at regular intervals to study whatever was brought before them for special consideration before being presented to the whole House for action.

50. Mary Patterson Clarke, *Parliamentary Privilege in the American Colonies* (New Haven, Conn., 1943), p. 132.

51. Rolland G. Usher, "The Institutional History of the House of Commons —1547–1641," in *Washington University Studies* (St. Louis, Mo., 1924), 11, no. 2 (1924):230–31.

The two committees in the Virginia Assembly consisted of eight men each, but Walter Shelley, a member of the first committee, died two days after being appointed and before the committee's work was completed. All members of the committees were burgesses, the "Counsell of Estate" having no part in their work.

Pory prepared a logical agenda for the assembly. First the delegates should consider the provisions of the "great charter of orders, lawes and privileges" to see if any points were absolutely out of harmony or entirely inconsistent with conditions in the colony, or in case "any lawe . . . did presse or binde too harde, that we might by waye of humble petition seeke to have it redressed; especially because this great charter is to binde us and our heyers for ever." Preliminary work, in this case, was referred to the two committees after Pory had broken the provisions of the charter into "fower books" for their easier study.

The second problem facing the assembly was to study all the instructions the Council of the Virginia Company had issued to the two previous governors and to the present one. They were to determine which instructions "might conveniently putt on the habite of lawes." Governor Yeardley suggested that he and the noncommittee members of the assembly study this matter. This was agreeable, and three hours of the first day were spent in discussing this problem.

To learn "what lawes might issue out of the private conceipte of any of the Burgesses, or any other of the Colony" was the third item Pory placed on the agenda for the assembly. And finally the members must decide "what petitions were fitt to be sente home for England."

Order of Business

The main work of the General Assembly of 1619 falls into three categories. First, that growing out of the charter sent by the company, which in reality amounted to a stamp of approval and a series of petitions for clarification or expansion of past promises or grants; second, a series of laws growing out of instructions sent from the Virginia Company to the governors in Virginia; and, third, a group of local laws for the better governing of the colony based, it seems, on common sense or, as Pory expressed it, "the private conceipte" of the members.

The "great Charter of lawes, orders and priviledges . . . had both the general assent, and the applause of the whole assembly," and Pory was commanded to express "their due and humble thankes to the Treasurer Counsell and company for so many priviledges and favours as well in their own names, as in the names of the whole Colony whom they represented." Among the petitions resulting from these laws was one requesting that a subtreasurer be sent to Virginia to collect rents, and that he be instructed to accept payment in commodities of the colony instead of specie (a problem which plagued colonial America until 1776). Another petition asked that workmen with various skills be sent "towards the erecting of the University and Colledge."

Of particular interest are the references made in this first assembly to the Indians of Virginia. During the dozen years the English had been settled in the New World the Indians had caused little trouble, but references in the assembly hint at a rising fear on the part of the English. A law was passed that "no injury or oppression be wrought by the English against the Indians whereby the present peace might be distrubed and antient quarrells might be revived."

Indians who came voluntarily to live and work with the English were to be watched carefully and, if possible, made to live separately in a house especially set aside for them. The assemblymen noted that "they are a most trecherous people and quickly gone when they have done a villany."

Any man who gave or sold ammunition or firearms to the Indians was liable to be tried for treason and, upon conviction, to be hanged. Any man who "purposely" went to any "Indian townes, habitations or places of resorte" without authority of the governor or the commander of the place where he lived, was to be fined forty shillings. All men except servants, however, were to be allowed to trade freely with the Indians.

Having anticipated trouble with the natives, the assembly undertook to eliminate potential causes. Inhabitants of the settlements were instructed "by just means" to take some of the most promising Indian children to be prepared "in the first elements of literature" so they would be qualified to attend the projected college. The Indians thus trained were then to be "sente to that worke of conversion." Christian Indians, the assembly believed, would be loving, peaceful, and friendly.

After having been studied by the noncommittee members of the assembly, instructions sent to the governors were referred in two parts to the two committees. From their report the assembly shaped a series of laws dealing with such varied topics as agriculture, relations with the Indians, the enforcement of contracts concerning tenants and servants, the sale of supplies and equipment, and the control and regulation of individuals in cases of idleness, gaming (particularly dice and cards), drunkeness, and "excesse in apparell."

Finally "a thirde sorte of lawes (such as might proceed out of every man's private conceipte)" was taken up and "referred by halves to the same committies which were from the beginning." These laws covered a variety of subjects—there were laws that prohibited selling or giving dogs "of the Englishe race" to the Indians, allowed no person to travel over twenty miles or a seven days' journey from an English settlement without permission from the governor, provided for a census and the keeping of other vital statistics, ordered the encouragement of religion, and required that persons passing Jamestown by water from one part of the colony bound for another should always stop to receive and deliver messages.

An interesting point to note about the procedure in the assembly is that all laws, before final passage, received three readings before the assembled representatives.

There seems to have been little if any notion of a bicameral legislative body in the organization of this assembly. Evidence, of course, is meager, but there is nothing in Pory's account of the action taken by the group to indicate that the council was in any way connected with the assembly in a capacity superior to that of the elected burgesses.

The General Assembly possessed not only legislative powers, but it also sat twice as a court. The English Parliament again was looked to for precedent in such action. In one case a servant was severely punished for "falsely accusing" his master, "impudently abusing his house," and for "bringing all his fellow servants to testifie on his side, wherein they justly failed him." Punishment was decided upon "by the general assembly (the governor himself giving sentence)." The second case was against Captain Henry Spelman who, at an Indian village, "spake very unreverently and maliciously" against Governor Yeardley. Such action was considered to be very serious and likely to increase friction between the Indians and the settlers. It was a threat to the peace that then existed but could have been easily broken. The outcome of this case, according to Pory's account, was that "Several and sharpe punishments were pronounced against him by diverse of the Assembly. But in fine the whole courte by voices united did encline to the most favorable, which was that for this misdemeanour he should first be degraded of his title Captaine at the head of the troupe and should be condemned to performe seven years service to the Colony, in the nature of Interpreter to the Governour."

The first tax levied in Virginia was passed on 4 August 1619, the final day of the first General Assembly.[52] In payment for their services to the assembly, Pory, the Speaker, John Twine, the clerk, Thomas Pierse, the sergeant, and the provost marshal of Jamestown, were to receive the receipts of this tax law. The fund was to be distributed to these men according to their degree and rank, which Pory understood. The tax law provided that "every man and manservant of above 16 yeares of age shall pay into the handes and Custody of the Burgesses of every Incorporation and plantation one pound of the best Tobacco." When collected, the tobacco was to be turned over to Pory to be distributed as directed.

The members of the General Assembly on the final day commended Pory for his "great paines and labour" as Speaker. It was he, they said, "who not onely first formed the same Assembly and to their great ease & expedition, reduced all matters to be treatted of into a ready method, but also, his indisposition notwithstanding, wrote or dictated all orders and other expedients, and is yet to write severall bookes for all the General Incorporations and plantations, both of the great charter, and of all the lawes."

Before concluding their business, the whole assembly directed Pory to "present their humble Excuse to the Treasurer, Counsell, and Company in England, for being constrained by the intemperature of the weather, and the falling sicke of diverse of the Burgesses, to breake up so abruptly, before they had so much as putt their lawes to the ingrossing." Pory was to copy "so many bookes of the same lawes as there be both Incorporations and Plantations in the Colony."

Concern was shown as to how the action of this assembly might be received in England. One of the final acts was a request to the treasurer, council, and company "that albeit it belongeth to them onely to allowe or to abrogate any lawes which we shall here inacte, and that it is their right so to doe; yet that it would please them not to take it in ill parte, if these lawes which we have nowe brought to light, do passe currant & be of force, till suche time as we may knowe their farther pleasure out of Englande: for other-

52. William Zebina Ripley, "The Financial History of Virginia," in *Studies in History, Economics and Public Law* 4, no. 1 (New York, 1893):18.

wise this people (who nowe at length have gotte the raines of former servitude into their owne swindge)[53] would in shorte time growe so insolent, as they would shake off all government, and there would be no living among them."

Having been in session six days, one of which was a Sunday on which no business was conducted, the assembly was prorogued by Governor Yeardley on Wednesday, 4 August 1619, until the first of March 1620.

The laws and petitions of the 1619 assembly were sent to England, but no record survives of the final action of the company. At an extraordinary court of the Virginia Company held on 20 March 1620, the laws were first mentioned. "The Acts of the general assembly in Virginia being yet to read," the record of the court shows, "because it was held inconvenient to spend an ordinary court therewith, it was agreed that Monday next in the afternoon should be appointed for that purpose." At an imperfect court held on 8 April 1620, Sir Edwin Sandys, treasurer, "signified that having perused the acts of the general assembly, he found them in their greatest part to be very well and judiciously carried and performed, but because they are to be ratified by a *great and general court*, therefore he hath writ unto them that till then they cannot be confirmed; but in the mean time he moved that a select committee of choice men might be appointed to draw them into head, and to ripen the business that it might be in readiness against the said court."[54]

In conformance with Sandys's suggestion a committee composed of four members of the council and four of the "generality" was appointed to organize the acts of the Virginia Assembly. This committee had power to adjourn and reconvene from day to day. At a later date another member was added to the committee, and the proceedings of the "imperfect court" were confirmed.

The final reference in the records of the Virginia Company to the laws passed in the colony was made at "a preparative court" held on 15 May 1620. "For the committee chose for the acts of the General Assembly," it reads, "Mr. Treasurer signified that they had taken extraordinary pains therein, but forasmuch as they were exceeding intricate and full of labour, he in their behalf desired the court to dispense with them till the quarter court in mid-summer term, which will be about six weeks hence, which the court with many thanks unto the committee for their great pains willingly

53. *Swindge* or *Swinge* is an obsolete term for "sway" or "power."
54. Hening, *Statutes*, 1:122.

assented unto."[55] During nearly two months the officers of the company were unable to decide what action to take on the laws passed by the Virginia Assembly during its brief six-day session, yet this was an assembly which the company had authorized. Clearly the company found it difficult to delegate power.

Original Records of the Assembly

The minutes of the Virginia General Assembly of 1619 which Pory kept were lost for over 230 years. As yet no *official* transcript of the proceedings has been found, and in all probability it was lost along with many other records of the Virginia Company. The first mention of a copy in England, however, occurs in a letter of 12 February 1620 from John Chamberlain to Sir Dudley Carleton. "Yesterday I received your letters by your nephew Dudley," he wrote, "but have not yet perused Master Pories parlement business, which I will impart to Sir D[udley] Diggs if he come to towne in any time."[56] Pory sent this account to Carleton, who was still ambassador at The Hague. It was taken by Marmaduke Rayner, an Englishman who was pilot of the Dutch man-of-war *Flushing*. This ship had come to Jamestown from the West Indies "in consort" with the *Treasurer* in September when she brought the first Negroes to the colony.[57]

The next mention of a record of the assembly is in the accounts of the courts of the Virginia Company between 20 March and 15 May 1620, cited by W. W. Hening in *The Statutes at Large . . . of Virginia*. Neither William Stith nor Thomas Jefferson met with any success in their efforts to locate an account of the first assembly.[58] After Hening's unsuccessful quest for the actual document in 1809, the matter rested until 1853 when Conway Robinson reported to the Virginia Historical Society that he had seen an original copy in the British State Paper Office.[59] Four years later George Bancroft wrote that "during a long period of years . . . partly in person and partly with the assistance of able and intelligent men" in the Public Record Office, he had made a search for and at last obtained the "Proceedings of the First Assembly in Virginia."

55. Ibid.
56. McClure, *Letters of John Chamberlain*, 2:287.
57. Alexander Brown, *The First Republic in America* (Boston, 1898), pp. 324–27.
58. Bancroft, "Introductory Notes," p. 333.
59. Tyler, *Narratives*, p. 248.

"The document is in the form of 'a reporte' from the Speaker," he noted, "and is more full and circumstantial than any subsequent journal of early legislation in the Ancient Dominion."[60] The copy found by Bancroft was published in the *Collections of the New-York Historical Society* in 1857. Later copies were made by Colonel Angus McDonald and D. C. De Jarnette. The De Jarnette copy was printed by order of the Virginia State Senate in 1874 in a thin pamphlet entitled *Colonial Records of Virginia, Senate Document Extra*. Lyon G. Tyler reprinted the text of this copy in his *Narratives of Early Virginia, 1600–1625*, published in 1907, and Susan M. Kingsbury followed the Tyler copy for her *Records of the Virginia Company*. A careful comparison of the various texts of this document printed in the United States reveals some variations of spelling and textual organization as well as a few variations in wording. In 1969 the Jamestown Foundation published these proceedings with a facsimile of Pory's original and a transcription on facing pages.[61]

No evidence has been found to indicate that another legislative assembly met in Virginia while Pory was secretary. In his *Statutes* Hening says that an assembly convened in November and December, 1621, according to brief references in the minutes of the Virginia Company, but Pory was then out of office. The work of this assembly dealt largely with measures recommended by the company for planting mulberry trees and encouraging the production of silk. The "acts" closed, Hening reported, with an enumeration of the wants of the colony.[62] Another General Assembly gathered in February 1624, but Pory's relationship to it was quite different from the one that he had held to the assembly of 1619.

Exploratory Voyages

While he retained his position in Virginia government Pory traveled on what might have been considered official business. He visited the Eastern Shore and made journeys of exploration north of the settled portion of the colony. After being replaced as secretary in November 1621 his travel seems to have been for pleasure, to satisfy his own curiosity about the country. He even penetrated

60. This, of course, is the copy sent by Pory to Carleton.
61. Edited by William J. Van Schreeven and George H. Reese, the *Proceedings* were published by the Jamestown Foundation with a brief introduction by Van Schreeven.
62. Hening, *Statutes*, 1:119.

the swampy wilderness south of Jamestown as far as the Chowan River in what is now North Carolina.

Eastern Shore

Before June 1620 Pory knew about the land on the ocean side of the Virginia peninsula known as the Eastern Shore. Tenants who were to be settled on Smith's Island just off the coast complained of their location, "saying there is no ground in all the whole Iland worth the manuringe." Pory described the Eastern Shore as "such a place to live . . . the like is skarce to be found againe in the whole country." It undoubtedly reminded him of his native fen country in Norfolk and Lincolnshire. He did not fail to mention however "the incomodity of Musquitos, which the ground being once cleared will vanish." "And for my particular," he added, "I was never so enamoured of any place."[63]

When the first ten tenants arrived to settle the plantation which the company had granted to the secretary's office in lieu of an established salary, Pory, at Yeardley's advice, took them over the bay to the Eastern Shore and personally selected the 500 acres of land assigned to his office.[64] The land which Pory selected is still known locally as Secretary's Plantation, and a white frame house there apparently built late in the eighteenth century but incorporating a much earlier dwelling, one brick end of which formed part of a wall facing the nearby water, was torn down about 1957.[65]

After he had settled his tenants and taken a muster to see that all were present and taken care of, Pory and Estinien Moll, not otherwise identified except as "a Frenchman," went over to Smith's Island where the salt works were then located. Having seen this part of the colony to his satisfaction, Pory returned to Jamestown.

Captain John Smith, in the fourth book of his *Generall Historie of Virginia, New England, and the Summer Isles*, included a section headed "The Observations of Master John Pory Secretarie of Virginia, in his travels." Rather than being a general account of

63. Pory to Sandys, 12 June 1620.
64. H. R. McIlwaine, ed., *Minutes of the Council and General Court of Virginia, 1622–1632, 1670–1676, with Notes and Excerpts from Original Council and General Court Records, into 1683, now Lost* (Richmond, Va., 1924), p. 148.
65. *Virginia, A Guide to the Old Dominion* (New York, 1940), p. 384. When I visited the site in the summer of 1968, residents of the neighborhood told me that the man who tore down the house used some of the material in a new house he was building in Norfolk, but they could not identify him for me.

his travels, however, this is a very detailed report on Pory's second trip to the Eastern Shore when he and his party visited several Indian towns. It deals with the honesty and frankness of the Indians as well as their treachery, with their government and their means of livelihood. Pory is revealed as a very keen observer and one who could tell an interesting story. It was at the Indian village of Onancock on this trip in 1621 that Pory is said to have been introduced to oysters and *batata* or "potatoes." After burning his mouth on a hot potato, Pory is traditionally reported to have said, "I would not give a farthing for a shipload."[66]

Chesapeake Bay and Potomac River

Before returning to Jamestown from this second trip to the Eastern Shore, Pory and his party continued north "into the great Bay," as they called the Chesapeake Bay, "where hee left setled very happily neare an hundred English, with hope of a good trade for Furres there to be had." They took no soundings of the bottom of the bay, intending to return later for that purpose.[67]

The treasurer and company in England on 25 July 1621, wrote to the governor and council in Virginia, "The voiadges and discoveries already made with the Land, as also uppon the Sea Coast, we highly Comend; and desire a constant course be held therein, for in that consistes the very life of the Plantation."[68] On 5 December, having heard of Pory's trip up the Potomac, the Virginia Company expressed pleasure over the "conjectures of the Southwest passage." "Since you now begin to discover the Cuntrie, and enquire after Comodities," they wrote, "we doubt not, but you shall find what you seeke or better."[69]

When Pory returned from his trip up the Potomac, he learned that he was no longer secretary in Virginia. Commissions to officers in the colony were granted "onely for three years in certain, and afterwards during the *Companies* pleasure."[70] The idea that he

66. Ibid., p. 379. The editor of the *Guide* was unable to give me the source of this tradition.

67. Edward Waterhouse, "A Declaration of the State of the Colonie and Affaires in Virginia. With a Relation of the barbarous Massacre in the time of peace and League, treacherously executed upon the English by the native Infidels, 22 March last," in Kingsbury, *Records of the Virginia Company*, 3:549.

68. Kingsbury, *Records of the Virginia Company*, 3:488.

69. Ibid., p. 544.

70. Force, *Tracts*, vol. 3, Tract No. 5.

might suddenly be thrown out of office at the end of three years had already occurred to Pory. In January 1620 he wrote, "The uncertainty of my being continued, or by some newe governour thrust out of my place, [shall not] any whitt dismay me from performance of my duty for the Interim; for that is a stroke, though many times unjust and cruell, for which there is no sense."[71]

On 13 June 1621 at the Trinity term quarterly court of the Virginia Company, Sir Francis Wyatt was chosen to succeed Yeardley in the governorship immediately upon the expiration of his present term. Having attended to the appointment of all other officials for Virginia, the court finally noted that "there remained now but one officer more of the council to be continued or changed, namely, Mr. Secretary Porey, whose commission, being but for three years, ended in November next." Members of the court were asked whether they desired to renew Pory's commission or to appoint another secretary. They indicated a desire for a change, and there were "four gentlemen proposed for the said place, namely, Mr. Smith, Mr. Paramore, Mr. Davison, and Mr. Waterhouse, being all of them recommended by worthy persons for their honesty, sufficiency and experience in secretary affairs."[72] Christopher Davison, eldest son of Sir William Davison, secretary of state under Queen Elizabeth, was chosen, "he having the major part of balls."[73] Davison, upon being informed of the decision, "did declare his thankful acknowledgement unto the company." The new secretary arrived at Jamestown in October 1621 while Pory was on his trip to the Eastern Shore and up the Potomac.

Having been relieved of all public duties, Pory was free to travel even farther afield into the inviting country around the settlements. To comply with the act of the General Assembly, he must have had approval from the governor since he traveled more than twenty miles from Jamestown and the other plantations. Very little was known about the interior of the country, particularly to the south. In 1609 John Smith had sent Michael Sicklemore, "a very honest, valiant, and painefull soldier," with two Indian guides to search for the colonists left by Sir Walter Raleigh in 1587 and to take note of the "silke grasse" growing in that part of the country. After three months Sicklemore returned from "Chawonock" and

71. Pory to Sandys, 13 Jan. 1620.
72. Brock, "Abstract of the Proceedings of the Virginia Company," 1:126–27.
73. Balloting in this case apparently followed the custom of using small black and white balls, with the voters being provided with one of each. They placed the ball indicating their choice in a box or urn. From this practice, of course, the term *to black ball* originated.

reported that he "found little hope and less certainetie" of the colony. Sometime later Nathaniel Powell and Anas Todkill were conducted "by the Quiyoughquohanocks" to the "Mangoages" on another search for the lost colonists but reported they could learn nothing except that they were all dead.[74] None of these men left any report on the country through which they passed.

Chowan River

In February 1622 Pory made an excursion into the same general area south of Jamestown "some 60. miles over land," he reported.[75] Pory's description of this new country along the Chowan River created a great deal of interest in England. On 18 April the Reverend Patrick Copland, who was vitally concerned with the proposed college in Virginia and later was chosen to be its rector, preached a sermon in Bow Church, London, that was published before the end of the year by order of the Virginia Company. Entitled *Virginia's God be Thanked, or a Sermon of Thanksgiving For the Happie successe of the affayres in Virginia this last yeare*, this book contains the first printed reference to Pory's explorations along the Chowan River. Copland knew of Pory's discoveries only a short time before because he had seen a letter (now lost) written from Virginia by George Sandys. Copland's sermon was preached within two months after the trip. Quoting in part from Sandys's letter, he said:

> Maister *Pory deserves good incouragement for his paineful Discoveries to the South-ward, as far as the Choanoack, who although he hath trod on a litle good ground, hath past through great forest*

74. Smith, *Generall Historie*, p. 87.
75. "A note of the Shipping, Men and Provisions Sent and Provided for Virginia . . . in the yeere 1621," in Kingsbury, *Records of the Virginia Company*, 3:641. Another report of the expedition says that Pory went fifty miles by land, but that the area he explored lay eighty miles by water (*A Perfect Description of Virginia* [London, 1649], p. 10. Pory may have had more than a passing interest in the rumors of survivors of the Roanoke colonists in this area, although his report apparently makes no mention of this. Pory's sister, Anne, was married to Robert Ellis; among the missing colonists were Thomas Ellis, adult, and Robert Ellis, a boy, conceivably relatives of Pory's brother-in-law. There possibly were other connections between Pory's family and some of the Roanoke colonists. There was a colonist named Chapman among the 1586 settlers, while Alis and John Chapman were among the "Lost Colonists" of 1587. The Reverend Joseph Mead in a letter to Pory, in care of his sister in Albermanbury, wrote, "Remember I pray my service to your good Sister & Mr. Chapman" (British Library, Harley Manuscripts, 383/67). There is no further indication of the relationship and it is not even clear whether Pory's sister was Mrs. Chapman.

of Pynes 15. or 16. myle broad and above 60. mile long, which will serve well for Masts for Shipping, and for pitch and tarre when we shall come to extend our plantations to those borders. On the other side of the River there is a fruitfull Countrie blessed with aboundance of Corne, reaped twise a yeere: above which is the Copper Mines, by all of all places generally affirmed. Hee hath also met with a great deale of silke grasse which growes there monethly of which Maister *Harriot*, hath affirmed in print many yeeres agoe, that it will make silke Growgraines. and of which and Cotten woll all the *Cambaya* and *Bengala* stuffes are made in the East Indies.

The Virginia Company's broadside, headed *A Note of the Shipping, Men and Provisions Sent and Provided for Virginia . . . in the yeere 1621*, published in 1622, reported substantially the same thing.

> In February last he likewise discovered to the South River, some 60. miles over land from us, a very fruitfull and pleasant Countrey, full of Rivers, wherein are two harvests in one yeere (the great King giving him friendly entertainment, and desirous to make a league with us) he found also there in great quantity of the same *Silke-grasse*, (as appeareth by the samples sent us) whereof Master *Heriott* in his booke 1587. makes relation, who then brought home some of it, with which a piece of Grogeran was made, and given to Queen Elizabeth, and some heere who have lived in the *East Indies* affirme, that they make all their *Cambaya* Stuffes of this, and Cotten-wooll.
>
> Also in his passage by land, Master *Porey* discovered a Countrey, full of Pine trees, above twenty miles long, whereby a great abundance of *Pitch* and *Tarre* may be made: and other sorts of woods there were, bit for *Pot-ashes* and *Sope-ashes*.
>
> The Indians have made relation of a Coper-mine, that is not far from thence, how they gather it, and the strange making of it: a piece whereof was sent home, being found (after triall) very excellent metall.

A pamphlet by Edward Waterhouse, *A Declaration of the State of the Colonie and Affaires in Virginia*, published the same year, included the same information. All three of these publications in 1622 probably drew upon the same source, perhaps an official report by Pory to the Virginia Company which is now lost.

The "silke-grasse" which so interested Pory and his contemporaries was *Yucca filamentosa* or bear grass, a plant from which the Indians made thread and string. Thomas Hariot described it as "a kind of grasse . . . upon the blades whereof there groweth very good silke in forme of a thin glittering skin to bee stript of[f]. It groweth two foote and a half high or better: the blades are about two foot in length, and half inch broad."[76] Queen Elizabeth is said to have had a gown made from the fibres of this plant.[77]

The samples of silk grass which Pory sent to the company delighted the officials. His "paines and discoveries" were highly praised. Perhaps forgetting in their excitement that they had declined to reappoint Pory to a second three-year term as secretary, the council of the company asked him to try to secure larger quantities of thread from the silk grass so that more accurate tests might be made of it.[78]

They were also pleased with the information Pory sent them on copper, and the promise it offered remained alive for many years. In 1649 an account was published that "Master Porye . . . reported the King there told him, that within ten days Journey Westward towards the Sun setting, there were a people that did gather out of a River sand, the which they washed in Sives, and had a thing out of it, that they then put into the Fire, which melted, & became like to our Copper, and offered to send some of his People to guide him to that place. But master Pory being not provided with men as he would have had of English, he returned to Sir George Yearly, and acquainted him with the Relation." The following year another tract repeated substantially the same information but cited "Mr. Poryes Narrative" to the Earl of Southampton as one of the sources for the information that "the Natives of the Countrey gathered a kinde of a Red Sand falling with a streame issuing from a Mountaine, which being washed in a sive, and set upon the fire speedily melts and becomes some Copper."[79] Clearly, a fuller account of Pory's discoveries was available then than is known now.

Nowhere in Pory's letters has even so much as a hint been found of the Indian massacre in Virginia on 22 March 1622. He had just returned from the Chowan River, and this great tragedy prevented him from returning with more men for a longer stay and a more extensive exploration.[80] Pory undoubtedly hesitated to spread the news of the massacre because of the damage that would

76. Thomas Hariot, *A Brief and True Report of the New Found Land of Virginia* (London, 1588) [Facsimile edition, no publisher, no date; not paged].

77. Force, *Tracts*, vol. 3, Tract No. 11. *Virgo Triumphans: or, Virginia richly and truly valued; more especially the South parte thereof: viz. The fertile Carolana and no less excellent Isle of Roanoak* (London, 1650), p. 16, reported that of this silk grass "Queene Elizabeth had a substantial and rich peece of Grograine made and presented to Her."

78. Council of Virginia Company to Governor and Council in Virginia, 10 June 1622, in Kingsbury, *Records of the Virginia Company*, 3:647.

79. *A Perfect Description of Virginia*, p. 10; *Virgo Triumphans*, p. 17.

80. *A Perfect Description of Virginia*, p. 10.

result to the colony if more information than was absolutely necessary reached prospective colonists in England. Yet if he made any confidential reports, even they have not been found.

Return to England

Sometime in the summer of 1622 Pory left Virginia aboard the *Discovery*,[81] commanded by Captain Thomas Jones, who is believed to have been the same Captain Jones who was master of the *Mayflower* in 1620.[82] The *Discovery* was in the service of a number of London merchants and was commissioned to discover all possible harbors between Jamestown and Plymouth, to explore the shoals of Cape Cod, and to trade with the coastal Indians wherever possible.[83]

Visit to New England

By August the *Discovery* had reached the young settlement at Plymouth. Pory, conditioned as a writer of newsletters, lost no opportunity to observe and later to record what he saw. His description of Plymouth was written by January 1623,[84] about seven years before William Bradford began writing his *History of Plimoth Plantation*. It is contained in two letters, one to the governor of Virginia, written probably in the late summer of 1622, and the other to Henry Wriothesley, Earl of Southampton and treasurer of the Virginia Company, completed soon after 13 January 1623. In 1918 Champlin Burrage edited and published these letters as *John Pory's Lost Description of Plymouth Colony in the Earliest Days of the Pilgrim Fathers*. Pory's letters, Burrage noted, contained such "a glowing account of Plymouth Plantation as might well have filled the hearts of the Pilgrim Fathers with pride, had they ever seen it." "Pory's narrative," he continued, "should no doubt carry all the more weight because it bears no sign of sectarian bias."[85]

Pory briefly reviewed the history of the Plymouth colony

81. *Collections of the Massachusetts Historical Society*, 9:16.

82. Alexander Young, *Chronicles of the Pilgrim Fathers of the Colony of Plymouth, from 1602 to 1625* (Boston, 1849), pp. 100, 298.

83. *Collections of the Massachusetts Historical Society*, 9:16.

84. Champlin Burrage, *John Pory's Lost Description of Plymouth Colony in the Earliest Days of the Pilgrim Fathers* (Boston, 1918), pp. 41–42.

85. Ibid., pp. xiv–xx.

ANNOTATIONS
UPON THE FOUR·TH BOOK
OF MOSES', CALLED

NUMBERS.

WHEREIN, BY CONFERENCE OF THE
SCRIPTVRES, BY COMPARING THE GREEK AND

Chaldee Verſions, and teſtimonies of Hebrew writers;
the Lawes and Ordinances given of old unto
Iſrael in this book, are explained.

By *Henry Ainſworth.*

I Will put you in remembrance, though ye once knew this, how that
the Lord having saved a people out of the land of Egypt, afterward destroyed them that beleeved not. Iude *v.5.*

Fourtie yeres was I grieved with this generation . Pſal. *95.10.*

But with whom was he grieved fourtie yeres? was it not with them that
had synned, whose carkeſſes fell in the wildernes? And to whom ſware he,
that they ſhould not enter into his reſt; but to them that beleeved not? So
wee ſee, that they could not enter in, becauſe of unbeleef. Let us
labour therfore to enter into that Reſt, leſt any man
fall after the ſame example of unbeleef.
Heb. *3, 17. 18.19. & 4.11.*

Imprinted·in the yere **1619.**

*The title page of one of Ainsworth's books mentioned by Pory in
his letter of 28 August 1622 to William Bradford. Bradford gave
Pory a copy to read on the voyage home.*

from the time of its sailing until it was well established, but he was most interested in the natural resources of the region around the settlement. He also commented upon the friendly relations existing between the colonists and the Indians, the threat of hostile French settlers, and the religious interests of the people. His observations on the Indian language are of particular interest. "Of the language of the natives about Plymmouth and Cape Cod," he wrote, "I have collected a small dictionarie, wherein I finde manie words agreeing with those of the South Colonie, and of the eastern shore of the bay."[86]

Before Pory left Plymouth, Governor Bradford gave him some books, perhaps to read on the long voyage to England. Pory's letter thanking the governor and William Brewster for their kindness to him and for the books, which he treasured as "juells," was dated 28 August, after the *Discovery* had sailed. He left in such haste that this point of courtesy had been neglected, he said. Pory signed himself "your unfained and firme friend," and it has been suggested that he may have been acquainted with both Bradford and Brewster when he was at The Hague while they were also in Holland.[87]

Shipwrecked in the Azores

Sometime late in the year the *Discovery* was driven off its course by storms and was wrecked in the Azores. Pory was seized by officials of these Portuguese islands and arraigned for piracy. It was even reported that he was in danger of being hanged.[88] He was imprisoned at Angra do Heroísmo, the capital of Terceira, one of the central islands of the group. It was while he was in the Azores that Pory wrote to Henry Wriothesley about what he had seen at Plymouth. The facts of his release are not known, but it has been suggested that plans for the marriage of the Prince of Wales and the sister of Philip IV of Spain may have produced an attitude of amiability on the part of the Portuguese officials in the islands toward their English prisoners.[89]

John Chamberlain sounded a pathetic note when he in-

86. Ibid., p. 44.
87. Edward D. Neill, *The English Colonization of America During the Seventeenth Century* (London, 1871), p. 153.
88. Chamberlain to Carleton, 26 July 1623, in McClure, *Letters of John Chamberlain*, 2:509.
89. *Collections of the Massachusetts Historical Society*, 9:16.

formed Sir Dudley Carleton of Pory's return to London. On 30 August 1623, he wrote, "Master Porie is come home very poore, and the best helpe he can get or hope for from his friends is to procure him protection from his old debts."[90]

[John Pory to Sir Dudley Carleton, 30 September 1619, Barlow Collection, New York Public Library.]

Right honorable and my singular good lorde,
Having mett with so fitt a messenger as this man of warre of Flushing, I could not but imparte with your lordship (to whom I am so everlastingly bounde) these poore fruites of our labours here; wherein though your lordship will espie many errors & imperfections, and matters of lowe esteeme; yet withall you wilbe contente to observe the very principle and rudiments of our Infant-Comonwealth; which though nowe contemptible, your lordship may live to see a flourishing Estate; maugre[91] both Spaniards & Indians. The occasion of this ships coming hither was an accidental consortship in the West Indies with the Tresurer an English man of warre[92] also, licensed by a Comission from the Duke of Savoye[93] to take Spaniards as lawfull prize. This ship the Treasurer wente out of England in Aprill was twelvemoneth, about a moneth, I thinke, before any peace was concluded between the king of Spaine & that prince. Hither shee came to Captaine Argall[94] then governor of this Colony, being parte-owner of her. Hee more for love of gaine the root of all evill, then for any true love he bore to this Plantation, victualled & manned her anewe, and sente her with the same Comission to raunge the Indies. The evente whereof (we may misdoubte) will proove some attempte of the Spaniard upon us, either by waye of revenge, or by way of prevention; least we might in time make this place sedem belli[95] against the West Indies. But our Governor being a soldier truly bred in that university of warre

90. McClure, *Letters of John Chamberlain*, 2:514.
91. "In spite of."
92. The *Treasurer* made a great many voyages to Virginia bringing colonists.
93. Charles Emmanuel I (1580–1630), one of four candidates for the throne of Bohemia.
94. Samuel Argall (d. 1626), first visited Virginia in 1609 and was afterwards there many times, most recently as governor from 1617 to 1619.
95. "The seat of war."

the lowe Countries, purposeth at a place or two upon the river fortifiable to provide for them, animating in the meane while this warlike people (then whom for their small number, no prince can be served with better) by his example to prepare their courages.

Both those of our nation and the Indians also have this Torride sommer bene visited with great sicknes & mortality; which our good God (his name be blessed for it) hath recompensed with a marvelous plenty, suche as hath not bene seen since our first coming into the lande. For my selfe I was partly at land & partly at sea vexed with a Calenture[96] of some 4. or 5. moneths. But (praised be god) I am nowe as healthfull as ever I was in my life. Here (as your lordship cannot be ignorant) I am, for faulte of a better, Secretary of Estate, the first that ever was chosen and appointed by Commission from the Counsell and Company in England, under their handes & common seale. By my fees I must maintaine my selfe; which the Governor telles me, may this yeare amounte to a matter of £300 sterling; wherof fifty I doe owe to himselfe, and I pray God the remainder may amounte to a hundred more. As yet I have gotten nothing, save onely (if I may speak it without boasting,) a general reputation of integrity, for having spoken freely to all matters, according to my conscience; and as neare as I could discerne, done every man right.

As touching the quality of this country, three thinges there bee, which in fewe yeares may bring this Colony to perfection; the English plough, Vineyards, & Cattle. For the first, there be many grounds here cleared by the Indians to our handes, which requireth an extraordinary deale of sappe & substance to nourish it: but of our graine of all sortes it will beare great abundance. We have had this yeare a plentifull cropp of English wheat, tho the last harvest 1618. was onely shed upon the stubble, and so selfe-sowne, without any other manurance. In July last so soon as we had reaped this selfe-sowne wheate, we sett Indian corne upon the same grounde, which is come up in great abundance; and so by this meanes we are to enjoye two crops in one yeare from off one & the same fielde. The greattest labour we have yet bestowed upon English wheate, hath bene, upon newe broken up groundes, one ploughing onely & one harrowing, far shorte of the Tilthe used in Christendome, which when we shall have ability enough to performe we shall produce miracles out of this earthe. Vines here are in suche abundance, as wheresoever a man treads, they are ready to embrace his foote. I have tasted here of a great black grape as big as a Damas-

96. "A burning fever."

cin,[97] that hath a true Muscatell-taste; the vine wherof now spending itselfe even to the topps of high trees, if it were reduced into a
vineyard, and there domesticated, would yeild incomparable fruite.
The like or a better taste have I founde in a lesser sorte of black
grapes. White grapes also of great excellency I have hearde to be in
the country; but they are very rare, nor did I ever see or taste of
them. For cattle, they do mightily increase here, both kine, hogges,
& goates, and are much greater in stature, then the race of them
first brought out of England. No lesse are our horses and mares
likely to multiply, which proove of a delicate shape, & of as good
spirite & metall. All our riches for the present doe consiste in
Tobacco, wherein one man by his own labour hath in one yeare,
raised to himselfe to the value of £200 sterling; and another by the
meanes of six servants hath cleared at one crop a thousand pound
English. These be true, yet indeed rare examples, yet possible to be
done by others. Our principall wealth (I should have said) con-
sisteth in servants: but they are chardgeable to be furnished with
armes, apparell, & bedding, and for their transportation, and cas-
uall[98] both at sea, & for their first yeare commonly at lande also:
but if they escape, they proove very hardy, and sound able men.
Nowe that your lordship may knowe, we are not the veriest beggers
in the worlde, our Cowe-keeper here of James city on Sundayes
goes acowtered all in freshe flaming silkes and a wife of one that in
England had professed the black arte not of a scholler but of a
collier of Croydon, weares her rough bever hatt with a faire perle
hattband, and a silken suite thereto correspondent. But to leave the
Populace, and to come higher, the Governor here, who at his first
coming, besides a great deale of worth in his person, brought onely
his sworde with him, was at his late being in London, together with
his lady, out of his meer gettings here, able to disburse very near
three thousand pounde to furnishe himselfe for his voiage. And
once within seven yeares, I am persuaded (absit invidia verbo)[99]
that the Governors place here may be as proffitable as the lord
Depuities of Irland. All this not withstanding, I may say of my selfe,
that when I was the last yeare with your lordship at Middleborough,
si mens non laeua fuisset,[100] I might have gone to the Hagh with
you, and founde my selfe there now in far better company, which
indeed is the soule of this life, and might have bene deeply ingrafted

97. "Damascus damson or plum."
98. Non-essentials.
99. "Let envy be absent from my speech," Livy, 9.19.15.
100. "If the mind had not been foolish," Vergil, *Eclogues*, 1.16.

into your lordships service, which since I have a thousand times affected in vaine. And therfore seing I have missed that singular happines, I must for what remaines, depend upon Gods providence, who, my hope is, wilbe so merciful towards me, as once more before I dye, to vouchsafe me the sight of your countenance, wherein, I speak unfainedly, I shall enjoye as muche happines as in any other thing I can imagine in this worlde. At my first coming hither the solitary uncouthnes of this place, compared with those partes of Christendome or Turky[101] where I had bene; and likewise my being sequestred from all occurrents and passages which are so rife there, did not a little vexe me. And yet in these five moneths of my continuance here, there have come at one time or another eleven saile of ships into this river, but fraighted with ignorance, then with any other marchandize. At length being hardned to this custome of abstinence from curiosity, I am resolved wholly to minde my busines here, and nexte after my penne, to have some good book alwayes in store, being in solitude the best and choicest company. Besides among these Christall rivers, & odoriferous woods I doe escape muche expense, envye, contempte, vanity, and vexation of minde. Yet Good my lorde, have a little compassion upon me, and be pleased to sende me, what pamphletts and relations of the Interim since I was with you, as your lordship shall thinke good, directing the same (if you please) in a boxe to Master Ralfe Yeardley Apothecary[102] (brother to Sir George Yeardley our governour) dwelling at the signe of the Hartychoke in great Wood-street,[103] to be sente to me by the first, together with his brothers thinges. This pacquett I delivered to one Marmaduke Rayner,[104] an Englishman, who goes intertained as Pilott in this Flemishe man of warre. If he come to your lordship, as he hath promised, he wilbe the fittest messenger. All possible happines I wishe to your lordship, and to my most honoured lady; and though remote in place, yet neare in affection, doe reste

Your lordships ever most humbly at your commaunde

101. Pory had been in Turkey from 1613 until 1616.

102. Yeardley, the apothecary, was a resident of the parish of St. Michael, Cornhill, London, as early as 1612. In 1642 he was chosen master of the Society of Apothecaries.

103. Wood Street in London extends from Cheapside (behind St. Paul's Cathedral) to Redcross and Fore Streets. The southern part was called Great Wood Street. This was not far from where Pory's sister lived.

104. Rayner's ship apparently is not identified by name in any of the surviving records of the Virginia Company. It was a ship of 160 tons. One Captain Jope was her commander on a voyage to the West Indies on one occasion when Rayner was pilot.

3. Final Years: Involvement with the Virginia Company ∿

The internal dissensions as well as outside forces that were shaking the Virginia Company to its foundations had been at work for some time before Pory's return to London in August 1623.[1] Sir Nathaniel Rich, Robert Rich (the Earl of Warwick), and Alderman Robert Johnson under the leadership of Sir Thomas Smyth had appealed to the king to order an investigation of the company from the time it came under the direction of Sir Edwin Sandys and his friends including Henry Wriothesley, Earl of Southampton, Nicholas and John Ferrar, and Sir John Danvers.[2] Their petition for an investigation, dated 23 April 1623, asked for the appointment of a commission with complete authority to inquire into the condition of the colony in Virginia in order to determine, among other things, the facts about certain alleged abuses and grievances or any wrongs and injuries done the adventurers and planters of the company. The commission should also be directed to suggest methods by which these wrongs might be corrected.[3] An appeal to the crown was in complete harmony with the accepted method of settling such mat-

1. Members of Parliament also anticipated action against the company even though in the House of Commons some ten percent of the members were stockholders (Robert E. Ruigh, *The Parliament of 1624, Politics and Foreign Policy* [Cambridge, Mass., 1971], pp. 123–24). This final phase in the history of the Virginia Company is discussed in several works. Wesley Frank Craven's *Dissolution of the Virginia Company* (New York, 1932) does so, of course, in considerable detail. Richard Morton's *Colonial Virginia* (Chapel Hill, N.C., 1960) covers it in a chapter entitled "Virginia Becomes a Royal Colony" (1:98–121), and Richard Beale Davis, in *George Sandys, Poet-Adventurer* (London, 1955), discusses Sandys's role in the investigation in Virginia in a chapter entitled "Colonial Official: The Active Life, 1622–1625," pp. 163–97. For an account sympathetic to Southampton see G. P. V. Akrigg, *Shakespeare and the Earl of Southampton* (Cambridge, Mass., 1968), pp. 158–65.

2. For a clear and concise sketch of the involved relationship of the parties concerned in this matter, see Thomas C. Johnson's introduction to *By the King: A Proclamation for Settling the Plantation of Virginia* (Charlottesville, Va., 1946).

3. "The humble Petition of Sundry the Adventurers and Planters of the Virginia and Sumer Iland Plantacons," in Susan M. Kingsbury, *The Records of the Virginia Company of London* (Washington, 1906–35), 2:373–74.

ters in those days when they could not be resolved through more ordinary means.

State of Affairs in the Virginia Company

On 24 May 1623, King James announced his plan to appoint such a commission. This, as the matter developed, was the first of three commissions involved in investigating and settling the affairs of Virginia. John Pory was a member of the second and third. The first, which King James mentioned on 24 May, was appointed in June and was composed of seven men headed by Sir William Jones. The investigation was to begin, not with the Sandys administration, but from the very first of Sir Thomas Smyth's going back to 1609.[4] Primarily the commissioners were to determine the current condition and needs of the plantations. On 25 June a letter from the king was read at a quarter court of the company in which he said that he expected a report from the commissioners within a few days and expressed his "will and pleasure" that the company not elect any new officers for two weeks.[5]

The Jones commission gleaned its information from mariners, former planters, and other persons, including Captain John Smith, who seemed to have any knowledge of the problems of the colony.[6] This haphazard means of gathering facts undoubtedly created a great deal of talk among all classes of people who had any interest at all in what was happening in Virginia. The air was so thick with rumors of impending change, that even the colonists in due time heard some of them. On 8 October the Privy Council issued the first of two orders designed to stabilize the situation both in the company and in the colony. A second order came on 20 October, and Pory was assigned the task of delivering both Privy Council orders in Virginia.[7]

The first of these set forth a new plan for the government of Virginia by a governor and twelve "assistants" residing in England and initially appointed by the king. Thereafter their successors would be elected by themselves from a list of persons approved by

4. Smyth had been one of the wealthy London merchants who provided financial assistance to Sir Walter Raleigh for his ill-fated colony of 1587.

5. Kingsbury, *Records of the Virginia Company*, 2:450–51.

6. For the seven questions which the commissioners asked John Smith and his answers to them, see John Smith, *The Generall Historie of Virginia* (London, 1624), pp. 165–68.

7. Public Record Office, CO 5/1354/199–200.

the king. There would also be a governor and twelve assistants residing in Virginia, who would be appointed by the governor and assistants in England with the approval of the king.[8] These provisions were to be incorporated into a new charter planned for the Virginia Company which the Privy Council termed a "new Company." The old charter was to be surrendered and the new one accepted in its stead. The company had either "to submit and surrender their former Charters and accept of a new Charter, with the alterations above mentioned," or else the king was determined "in default of such submission to proceed for the recalling of the said former charters in such sort as shall be just."[9]

The second of the two Privy Council orders was intended to calm the doubts of the Virginia planters and to offer them assurance that in whatever action was taken against the Virginia Company, their personal interests would not be compromised. Ships ready to sail momentarily with supplies for Virginia were ordered to proceed with "all speed . . . without any stop or delay." In the light of the final outcome of the proceedings against the company certain sections of this order are especially interesting:

> there is no other intention then meerly and only the reforming and change of the present Government, whereof His Majesty hath seen so many bad effects, as will tend to the endangering of the whole planation if it continue as is. Nevertheless forasmuch, as it concerns the publick Interests of many men, His Majesty's Royall care is such, that no man shall receive any prejudice but shall have his Estate fully and wholy conserved, And if in anything it be defective better to be secured, so as they need not apprehend any such fear, or other inconvenience, but contrarywise chearfull to proceed.[10]

This order was "thought fit to be published in the Company." From it, fully six months before a final decision was handed down, the Sandys party must have guessed what might have been the outcome of the proceedings against the company.

"Their Lordships think fitt," the order concluded, "that this and the two Annexed Orders of the Board [the orders of October 8 and 20] be Published by the bearer hereof Mr. John Porey, in all

8. This suggests James's familiarity with the government of the Cittie of Raleigh on Roanoke Island in 1587 which also provided for a governor and twelve assistants, some of whom remained in England. It may, of course, have been Sir Thomas Smyth whose memory was responsible for this arrangement.

9. Alexander Brown, *The First Republic in America* (Boston, 1898), pp. 550–52.

10. Privy Council Order, 20 October 1623. Public Record Office, CO 5/1354, Virginia Entry Books of Letters, Commissions, etc., 1606–62.

such places within Virginia, as hee shall think fit for the satisfaction of the Planters there."

Commission of 24 October 1623

A second commission appointed to inquire into the state of affairs in Virginia was appointed by the Privy Council on 24 October 1623. Its members were John Harvey, John Pory, Abraham Piersey, Samuel Matthews, and John Jefferson.[11] This body, like the others concerned with the affairs of Virginia, held a temporary commission. It was instructed to "make a diligent enquiry of those particulars following," because its members were "well acquainted with the Courses and Conditions" in Virginia:

> How many severall Plantations there bee, and which of them publique and which private and particular: what people, men, women and children be in each Plantation. What fortifications or what place is best to be fortifyed. What Houses and how many; what Cattle, what Arms, Ammunition and Ordnance mounted and serviceable; what Corn and other provisions of Victualls, what Boates and Barques, what Bridges and publique works, how the Colony standeth in respect of the Savages, what Hopes may be truly and really conceived of that Plantation; And lastly the directest means to attain to those hopes.[12]

On the same day this commission was appointed, the Privy Council also wrote the governor and council in Virginia explaining their action and requiring officials there to "yeald them your best ayde and assistance upon all occasions and in all those things wherin they shall find cause to use the same to the end aforesaid."[13]

Harvey and Pory, the only members of the commission not already in the colony, reached Virginia probably late in February 1624. Pory immediately publicized the Privy Council's orders.[14] Warrants had been issued about 26 January for the election of a General Assembly, and it was in session when the commissioners

11. W. L. Grant and J. Monro, eds., *Acts of the Privy Council, Colonial Series* (London, 1908), 1:71–72. From the records available it seems that Jefferson alone of the five commissioners never took any part in the investigation.

12. Order in Council, 24 October 1623. Bancroft Transcripts (New York Public Library), 2:205–7.

13. *Acts of the Privy Council of England, 1623–1625* (London, 1933), p. 108.

14. In a letter to the governor and General Assembly dated 2 March 1624 the commissioners referred to the publishing of the Privy Council's order the week before (Public Record Office, CO 1/3/2).

gathered in Virginia. Both the assembly and the commissioners seem to have lost no time in settling down to the business at hand.

Investigation in Virginia

On 2 March all of the commissioners except Jefferson (who remained aloof) joined in sending a "briefe declaratione" to the governor and the General Assembly in which they set forth their purpose (to obtain "an exact accompt of the present Estate of this Colony in divers Considerable respects") and asked for advice and assistance. They opened the way for suggestions as to how they might best accomplish their mission.[15]

The assembly proved to be uncooperative. It did, nevertheless, issue an order that "the several Plantations shall transporte the Commissioners sent over by his Majesty's Privie Counsell from Plantation to Plantation according to their desire," and it was directed that the men be accommodated "in the best state theire Howses and Roomes will afforde."[16]

The second day of March 1624 must have been a very busy day indeed for both the General Assembly and the commissioners. While it is impossible to determine the exact sequence of events on that day, it appears that the "briefe declaratione" was sent to the assembly first. It was followed by a second letter from the commissioners requesting that some definite course of action be planned for the accomplishment of their mission. They sent a "forme" with their letter for the members of the assembly to sign, it "being none other then wee ourselves will most readely and most humbly sett our hands unto."[17]

This "forme of Subscription" which the commissioners hoped to induce the members of the General Assembly to sign was unreasonable, in view of the fact that the assembly had already demonstrated a reluctance to cooperate. Dated simply March 1624, with a space left blank for the specific day, it read,

> Whereas out of theire Lordships three Orders from the Counsell board in England lately published in this General Assembly, we are given to understand, that his Majesty hath signified his gratious pleasure for the universall good of this Plantation (now by

15. Kingsbury, *Records of the Virginia Company*, 4:464–65.
16. H. R. McIlwaine, ed., *Journals of the House of Burgesses of Virginia, 1619–1658/9* (Richmond, Va., 1915), p. 41.
17. Public Record Office, CO 1/3/3.

reason of our late calamaties being in an unsettled estate) to institute another forme of Government, whereby this worke may be
upheld and better prosper in time to come, and to that end hath
required surrender of the present Pattents, declaring neverthelesse
his Majesty's Royal resolution of assuringe unto the particular
members of the Company such Lands and priviledgs in the said
Cuntrie, as according to the proportion of each mans adventure,
and proper interests do now belong unto them. Wee of this general
Assembly do by subscription of our names not only professe and
testifie our due thankfullness for that his Majesty's most gratious
and tender care over us, but do for our parts in all humility and
willingnes submit ourselves to his princely pleasure of revoking the
ould Pattents, and of vouchsafeinge his Majesty's new Letters
Pattents, to those noble ends and purposes above mentioned.[18]

The letter transmitting this subscription to the assembly
concluded, "At your service towards the setting upp of the Publique." The governor, council, and General Assembly all united to
reply to the commissioners about the document that had been
submitted for their signature. On 2 March, the same date it was
received, they wrote, "Wee have presented our humblest thanks to
his sacred Majesty for this gratious and tender care over us and
have returned our answers (in due submissions) to theire Lordships
Letters and Orders. When our consent to the surrender of the
Pattents, shalbe required, will be the most proper time to make
reply: in the mean time wee conceive his Majesty's intention of
changeing the Government hath proceeded from much misinfor-
mation, which wee hope may be altered uppon our more faithfull
declarations."[19]

The stage was set in Virginia for that phase of the disagreement between the two factions in the Virginia Company leadership
with which the people there were concerned. Standing ready to
oppose the efforts of John Harvey, John Pory, Abraham Piersey,
and Samuel Matthews were the governor, Sir Francis Wyatt; his
council and the General Assembly, composed of Francis West,
George Sandys, Sir George Yeardley, and others including Ralph
Hamor, a former secretary; and three men who had been members
of the 1619 assembly.

The General Assembly suspected the commissioners of having secret instructions of some sort, perhaps to trick them into
signing away the liberty which had come to the colony through Sir
George Yeardley's instructions in 1619. On that eventful second
day of March, the day before adjournment, the assembly asked the

18. Ibid.
19. Public Record Office, CO 1/3/4.

commissioners to "shew us the depth of your Authority: or otherwise to sett itt downe under your hands that youe have no further Commission or Instructions which may concern us as you have already professed." Just as the commissioners had closed their earlier letter, the Assembly now signed theirs "Ready to joyn with you for the Publique."[20]

The commissioners promptly informed the governor and assembly that they had no authority or instructions to force the signing of the subscription which had been drawn up, but that "the marke aimed att was no lesse then his Majesty's favor uppon our persons and comon cause to be obteyned by obedience and thankfullness." The commissioners frankly admitted, however, that they could not "professe that we have no further Comission which may concern youe . . . for our Comission yett unperformed concerneth youe in your persons, servants, Corne, Cattle, armes, houses, &c. Nor need you suspect that wee will attempt any thinge to the wrong of any man, or which wee cannot very well Answer."[21]

To get on with the business for which they had been sent to Virginia, the commissioners submitted four questions to the governor and assembly in order to obtain their opinions on the matters in which the Privy Council was interested. The commissioners were anxious to know

> 1. What places in the Cuntrie are best or most proper to be fortified or maintained either against Indians or other enemies that may come by sea?
> 2. How the Collony now stands in respect of Savadges?
> 3. What hopes may truly and really be conceived of this Plantation?
> 4. And lastly which be the directest meanes to attaine to these hopes?[22]

The General Assembly very obligingly replied to the four questions and as a whole painted a rosy picture of conditions in Virginia. Although no lives had been lost because of unfriendly Indians since the massacre of 22 March 1622, Indian relations still constituted one of the major problems facing the colonists. It was largely of the "inconveniencyes" of having to "watch and warde to secure our selves and labors" that the assemblymen complained. They described Virginia as "one of the goodlyest partes of the earth" and cited a great many of the same advantages and features which Pory himself had written about a few years earlier. To attain

20. Public Record Office, CO 1/3/5.
21. Public Record Office, CO 1/3/6.
22. Public Record Office, CO 1/3/2.

the hopes of Englishmen for a flourishing colony in Virginia, the assembly suggested a "runninge armye continually a foote to keepe the Indians from settlinge on any place that is neere us," and, as Pory also had advocated earlier, that new settlers arrive in the middle of winter with provisions to last a year; that qualified men be sent to manage vineyards and mulberry trees and to plant gardens and orchards; and that "the wealth of the mountaines and Comodities of the Seas" be discovered and used. They also repeated a number of other suggestions that had been made in the past for improving conditions in the colony. All in all, the assembly's reply to the four questions must have been of little use to the commissioners in their search for new suggestions for improving Virginia.[23]

Before the commissioners had completed their investigation for the Privy Council the General Assembly "demanded" to know what they were going to report, but this demand was rejected. The commissioners replied that the Privy Council was to see their report first. The assembly, "having the same care," attempted to keep to itself whatever information it might have been able to give the commissioners, but in this they "were prevented by Mr. Porye . . . who contrary to his professed integritie, Hath suborned the Clarke of our Counsell with reward and promises to betray our Secrecye, and to geve him Copies of all our proceedings."[24]

When Christopher Davison, the secretary who succeeded Pory in 1622, died in the winter of 1623–24, his clerk, Edward Sharpless, took over the duties of the office as acting secretary.[25] Stith, whose history of Virginia was first published in 1747, reported that a copy of an oath administered to Sharpless when he took over the secretary's duties, was then among the public records of the colony.[26] By this oath he was required to say nothing of matters "treated secretly at the Counsell table" and not to "deliver any thing concerninge that affayres of the Counsell to any other person to be copied out or engrossed without first making the Governour acquainted and pleasure obtained."[27]

Officials of the government in Virginia at a court held 10 May 1624, tried Sharpless for yielding to Pory's "promise of re-

23. Public Record Office, CO 1/3/7.
24. Council in Virginia to the Earl of Southampton and the Council of the Company of Virginia, 12 May 1624, in Kingsbury, *Records of the Virginia Company*, 4:481.
25. Ibid., 1:46.
26. William Stith, *The History of the first Discovery and Settlement of Virginia* (London, 1753), p. 315.
27. Edward D. Neill, *Virginia Carolorum: The Colony Under the Rule of Charles the First and Second, A. D. 1625–A. D. 1685* (Albany, N.Y., 1886), p. 26.

ward, &c." and "giveing copyes of our workings & Letters to the Kings Majesty & the Lords of the privye Counsell, to some of the Commissioners." By "sufficient proofe & his own confession" Sharpless was found guilty and sentenced to be "sett upon the pillory in the Market place of James Citty, & there to have his eares nayled to it, & cutt of[f].[28] The sentence was later reduced, however, and he lost only a piece of one ear and was returned to his former status as an indentured servant.[29]

The court, before adjourning, also ordered a letter to be sent to the Virginia Company explaining Pory's part in this incident and telling them of the punishment meted out to Sharpless.[30] From Pory's action, they wrote to Henry Wriothesley, Earl of Southampton, who was a leading member of the Virginia Company Council, they began to "Suspect some Synister intentione" and wanted him to understand Pory's "duble dealinge" so that he might attempt to "prevent his practises." The council members in Virginia also hoped that the Privy Council would "give smale Creditt to any his particuler informations, which agree nott with the generall, The Acte arguinge faction and noe way becominge the service."[31]

When the assembly discovered that copies of their reports had reached the commissioners it immediately dispatched "a letter, petition, and other things . . . partly to his Majesty and partly to the Lordes [of the Privy Council],"[32] by a special messenger, John Pountis, who thereby gained the distinction of being the first appointed agent of the colony to the mother country.[33] Pountis, however, died at sea, and the reports which he carried did not serve to counteract any adverse report from the commissioners.

Since the commissioners did not complete their investigation until about the middle of April 1624, it seems likely that they visited other settlements as well as Jamestown. There can be no doubt that they gathered an accurate consensus on the subject from

28. The manuscript Court Book of the Colony, 10 May 1624, Library of Congress.

29. M. R. McIlwaine, ed., *Minutes of the Council and General Court of Colonial Virginia, 1622–1632, 1670–1676, with Notes and Excerpts from Original Council 2nd General Court Records, into 1683, now Lost* (Richmond, Va., 1924), p. 52.

30. The manuscript Court Book of the Colony, 10 May 1624, Library of Congress.

31. Kingsbury, *Records of the Virginia Company*, 4:481.

32. John Harvey to Sir Nathaniel Rich, 24 April 1624, in Kingsbury, *Records of the Virginia Company*, 4:476–77.

33. Ella Lonn, *The Colonial Agents of the Southern Colonies* (Chapel Hill, N.C., 1945), p. 7.

the whole colony. Not everyone in Virginia agreed with the governor and assembly that local affairs under the recent direction of the Virginia Company had been properly managed.

Pory, whom Harvey considered an "understanding and well furnisht . . . messenger," left Virginia soon after 24 April taking with him the report of the commission. Harvey wrote that he was remaining in Virginia "till my ships retourne from Cannada, after which time, if god keep mee alive having been wintered and somered heere, you shall knowe my opinion of the place to the full."[34] The other two commissioners, Samuel Matthews and Abraham Piersey, remained in Virginia and within four months after Pory's departure had become members of the council. Pory arrived in London early in June, accompanied by the governor's wife, Lady Margaret Wyatt, "great with child."[35]

On 11 June Pory delivered to Sir Nathaniel Rich an account of the report of the commissioners which had been prepared in Virginia. This report was objective and honest and in no wise unfair either to the Virginia Company or to the colonial administration. Yet in a document issued a month later over the king's signature facts alleged to have come from the commissioners were set forth which were quite opposite to those in the account that Pory delivered to Rich. The commissioners reported "the persons heer to bee more in number, and provisions of victualls to bee more plentifull then wee expected."[36] Yet on 15 July 1624 a document issued by the king said in part that the commissioners from Virginia "did certifye us that our subjects and people sent to inhabite there . . . Were most of them by Godes visitation sicknes of bodye famyne and by massacres . . . by the native Savages of the lande dead and deceased."[37] It is entirely possible, of course, that such a report was secretly drawn up and delivered to the king.

The letter from Harvey which Pory delivered stressed the need of freeing the people from the fear of Indian raids, after which "the plantation with good government would undoubtedly flourish." Yet the king cited the commissioners as having "conceived [the country] to be fruitfull and healthfull after our people had

34. Harvey to Rich, 24 April 1624, in Kingsbury, *Records of the Virginia Company*, 4:476–77.

35. Chamberlain to Carleton, 19 June 1624, in Norman E. McClure, *Letters of John Chamberlain* (Philadelphia, Pa., 1939), 2:566.

36. Harvey to Rich, 24 April 1624, in Kingsbury, *Records of the Virginia Company*, 4:476. Craven, *Dissolution of the Virginia Company*, pp. 325–26.

37. James I, "Commission to Certain Lords of the Privy Council and others for Settling a Government in Virginia, 15 July 1624" in Kingsbury, *Records of the Virginia Company*, 4:493.

beene some tyme there and that if industrie Were used it Woulde produce many staple and good comodities though as yet the sixteen yeres govermente now past [that is, Sir Edwin Sandys's administration] had yeilded fewe or none and that this neglect they conceived must fall on the governors and Company here whoe had power to directe the plantations there."[38]

Most of the men in Virginia had been pleased with Sir Edwin Sandys's administration of the company and especially with the new freedom they enjoyed in their own government. If Pory delivered to the king the information James claimed to have received from the commissioners, no record of it has been found. Quite the contrary, the surviving documents reflect local feeling as being the "most bitter invectives in the highest pitche of spleen and detraction, against the twelve yeares goverment of Sir Thomas Smith." Yet Pory may well have been the tool of King James and of the Smyth-Warwick faction that he was suspected of being in Virginia.[39]

The king and Privy Council, however, were in no position by this time to publish anything favorable to Virginia. The case against the Virginia Company had already been decided and the charter declared vacated on 24 May 1624, several weeks before Pory returned to London. A writ of *quo warranto* had been issued from King's Bench the previous 4 November, and the decision (against Sir Edwin Sandys's leadership) was issued in May under which the king assumed the privileges of the company.[40] It was in 1624 that James, probably feeling quite powerful, boasted, "I have broken the Necks of three Parliaments, one after another."[41] He might also have counted the young parliament of Virginia among his temporary conquests.

Pory petitioned the Privy Council to reimburse him £100 which he had spent in connection with the investigation in Virginia, but, "forasmuch as wee find that he hath taken paines and used diligence in the performance of the said service," it was recom-

38. Ibid.
39. Harvey to Rich, 24 April 1624, in Kingsbury, *Records of the Virginia Company*, 4:476. The letter of Joseph Mead to Sir Martin Stuteville, 8 October 1624, quoting Pory at length, reports that Pory had been to Harwich to see Warwick, and that the Earl had sent Pory to the court, then at Wilton and Salisbury, and that Pory returned with letters for Warwick.
40. Craven, *Dissolution of the Virginia Company*, pp. 315–18. Kingsbury, *Records of the Virginia Company*, 4:358–98.
41. John Rushworth, ed., *Historical Collections of Private Passages of State, Weighty Matters in Law, Remarkable Proceedings in Five Parliaments, Beginning the Sixteenth Year of King James, Anno 1618* (London, 1659), 1:140.

mended that he be given £150.[42] On 20 July he received that amount as a "Princely reward for the said service & without accompt imprest or other Chardge to bee sett upon him or his assignes for the same or for anie parte thereof."[43] It is entirely possible that this "Princely reward" and generous protection from old creditors was in the nature of a bribe to prevent him from revealing the true state of affairs in Virginia. For example, in June 1625 the council in Virginia wrote, "It is no new thinge to us to be wronged by the defamatione of malitious rumors . . . and we wounder that such a rumor should goe uncontrolde when Mr Porye . . . was present at the fynell conclusione of that busines, and coulde have certified the contrarie."[44]

The other members of the commission also received kindly treatment under the new administration. In addition to the appointment of Matthews and Piersey to the Council in Virginia, Harvey became governor and Pory, himself, was added to a new commission resident in England for managing the affairs of Virginia.

Commission of 15 July 1624

King James on 15 July 1624 issued a commission to certain members of the Privy Council and a few others for settling the affairs of the Virginia Company and establishing a new government for the colony. The personnel of this commission, of which Pory was a member (but which for the most part was merely the Privy Council sitting as a commission),[45] was under the close scrutiny of James. Any six of the more than fifty members could conduct business provided one of the six was one of eight men whom the king specifically listed. James also took an active part in later changes in membership. Once, for example, he insisted on the appointment of a Mr. Bing whom the commissioners considered only "a mere good fellow," and who would have delayed any business in which he took part.[46] In August, after the matter had been taken up with the king, Pory was "sent back" with the

42. *Acts of the Privy Council of England, 1623–1625*, p. 276.
43. "Warrant to Pay John Pory, 20 July 1624" in Kingsbury, *Records of the Virginia Company*, 4:500.
44. "Council in Virginia to the Commissioners for the Affairs of Virginia, June 15, 1625," in Kingsbury, *Records of the Virginia Company*, 4:563.
45. Kingsbury, *Records of the Virginia Company*, 1:111.
46. Thomas Conventrye to Sir Edward Conway, 25 July 1624, Bancroft Transcripts, New York Public Library, 2:501–503.

commission to have "Mr. Pottes his name out of it."[47] And finally James told the commission to employ James Stuart in "such wayes of imployment, as may bee most fitt for him" because of his "industrie, zeale, and good affection."[48]

The commission from James began with a recital of the events leading up to the appointment of this new group and included information from the apparently much-altered report that Pory was alleged to have brought back from his investigation of the colony. James expressed great concern for the welfare of his subjects in Virginia and gave the new commissioners specific instructions about their duties which were to continue until he chose to "signify his pleasure to the contrary."[49]

By the king's grant these commissioners were given all the powers formerly vested in the Virginia Company: authority to issue orders and directions for sending supplies to the colony by whatever means they could devise; to call together adventurers or planters for the advancement of the colony or to appoint committees for the well-being of the colony; full freedom "to consulte consider of propose and sett downe all such matters and things most necessarie and convenyente for the settling and establishing of the govermente" in Virginia; to control trade and traders to and from the colony; to work out the provisions "necessarye to be incerted in the newe Charter by us intended to be made for the good of the saide plantation and Colony"; as well various other specific grants. To aid them in carrying out these duties, James ordered that "all bookes orders letters advises and other Writinges and thinges in any Wise concernying the said Colony and Plantation in whose handes so ever the same be" were to be turned over to this new commission.[50]

The day following their appointment more than twenty of the new commissioners, among whom was Pory, gathered at Sir Thomas Smyth's house to begin their new job. Careful plans were laid for their work. It was agreed that all who were "not of the quorum" should constitute a standing committee to prepare the order of business for the six or more commissioners who were

47. Earl of Warwick to Secretary Conway, 9 August 1624, Bancroft Transcripts, New York Public Library, 2:521–22.

48. The King to the Commissioners and Company of Virginia, 28 November 1624, Bancroft Transcripts, New York Public Library, 2:545–46.

49. W. Noel Sainsbury, ed., *Calendar of State Papers, Colonial Series, America and the West Indies, 1675–1676* (London, 1893), pp. 64–66.

50. "Commission to Certain Lords of the Privy Council and Others for Settling a Government in Virginia, 15 July 1624," in Kingsbury, *Records of the Virginia Company*, 4:490–97.

handling the affairs. All "Charters, Bookes and other writings" of the Virginia Company were ordered delivered to them; a committee was designated to report on current conditions in the colony and to plot a tentative course of action; and they very wisely detained all ships about to sail for Virginia until a report could be sent showing some progress in the interests of the colonists to allay their fears of great and sudden changes in the government.[51]

On 31 July Solicitor General Sir Robert Heath requested royal approval of the commission's plans to grant authority to some of the "principall Inhabitants" of Virginia to set up an interim government.[52] The work of the commission proceeded slowly and not according to its early plans. Finally at the death of King James on 27 March 1625, all of the commission's activities ceased.

Final Years

Pory probably spent most of the remainder of his active life in London, continuing his old profession of newsletter writer. He corresponded with the Reverend Joseph Mead, a versatile and renowned scholar who was about his own age; with Sir Thomas Puckering, a former member of Parliament and friend of the royal family; with young John, Viscount Scudamore, whose career at home and abroad lay in the future; and occasionally with Sir Thomas Lucy and Sir Robert Greville, Lord Brooke. His last known letter, dated 24 January 1633, was addressed to Puckering.[53]

On 3 October 1635, from Petworth in Sussex the Reverend George Garrard, a relative of Lady Carleton, wrote Sir Thomas

51. "Commissioners for Virginia: Orders Set Down at a Metting, 16 July 1624," in Kingsbury, *Records of the Virginia Company*, 4:497–500.

52. Sir Robert Heath to Edward Conway, 31 July 1624, Bancroft Transcripts, New York Public Library, 2:505–7. In 1629 Heath himself received a grant for a vast tract of land just south of Virginia which was named Carolana.

53. Pory apparently was succeeded as a writer of newsletters by Edward or Edmund Rossingham, nephew of Pory's first cousin, Temperance Flowerdew Yeardley, and hence also a relative of Pory's. Rossingham had been in Virginia and served as a member of the 1619 assembly representing Flowerdew Hundred. The last known newsletter from Pory's pen was addressed to Sir Thomas Puckering, 24 January 1633; before the end of the year Rossingham was writing regularly to Puckering and continued to do so as long as Sir Thomas lived (Yardley, *Before the Mayflower*, 257–60, in which Rossingham is called Edmund; Thomas Birch, ed., *The Court and Times of Charles the First* [London, 1849], 2:228, where Rossingham is called Edward). His letters apparently were signed with initials only. In 1619 at Jamestown Rossingham was referred to as ensign, but in 1622 he was addressed as captain. The following year he apparently was in London, as he was questioned concerning the charter of the Virginia Company (Kingsbury, *Records of the Virginia*

Wentworth that John Pory had recently died in London.[54] This quite clearly was a premature report, however. Attempts to discover a record of his burial in London parish registers have been fruitless, although a number of the registers were burned in the Great Fire of 1666. Apparently he left no will as no trace of one can be found in any of the courts to which it might have been submitted for probate.

The Bishop's Transcript of the Sutton St. Edmunds parish registers in Lincolnshire, however, contains the entry in 1636 that "Old John Pory was buryed the Two and Twentieth day of March." It was signed by Curate Thomas Watton and two of the churchwardens. The Prerogative Court of Canterbury on 4 April 1636, granted administration of the estate of this John Pory to his sister, Anne Ellis, wife of Robert Ellis.[55] Pory was described as "nuper de Sutton Sancti Edmundi in comitatu Lincoln, celebis." No earlier John Pory of Sutton St. Edmund is known who might have been described as *celebis* ("celebrated or well known"); Garrard was clearly misinformed when he reported Pory's death the previous October, yet none of his surviving letters to Wentworth contain a correction. If *nuper de Sutton Sancti Edmundi* ("recently of Sutton St. Edmund") is considered in a narrow sense it might be interpreted as meaning that Pory had only recently moved there. Members of the Pory family, nevertheless, had lived in this parish for more than three centuries, although there is no conclusive evidence to connect John Pory with any of them, not even with Anne Pory Ellis.[56] Yet

---

Company, 2:43; 3:154, 159; 4:116, 184, 186, 211). Between 1621 and 1624 he was frequently in Holland as Yeardley's factor for the sale of his Virginia tobacco, shipped to him there (Charles M. Andrews, *The Colonial Period of American History* [New Haven, Conn., 1938], 4:17). The Edward Rossingham who in December 1611, was steward to Sir John Digby, ambassador to Spain, and who returned to England a year later because of the death of his wife, may have been the father of the newsletter writer (McClure, *Letters of John Chamberlain*, 1:326, 397). This Rossingham may also be identified as the one of that name who was "sewer" (the officer who set and removed dishes, tasted the food, etc.) to the king in 1612 (Historical Manuscripts Commission, *Report on the Manuscripts of the Marquess of Downshire* [London, 1938], 3:400).

54. The original letter is in the Central Library, Sheffield, England (Str 15/232). It was printed in William Knowler, ed., *The Earl of Strafforde's Letters and Despatches with an Essay Towards His Life by Sir George Radcliffe* (London, 1739), 1:468.

55. Public Record Office. Act Books: Administrations. Prob. 6/15/161.

56. One Robert Ellice appears in the Sutton St. Edmunds register as chapelwarden in 1626, but he apparently could not write, as he signed records with his mark. Another John Pory whose will was dated 20 December 1681 and proved 6 April 1686 left property to the local churchwardens to support two commemorative sermons each year.

St. Edmund's Church, Sutton St. Edmunds, Lincolnshire, where Pory is buried. This ancient church was rebuilt in 1795.

the parish register contains a record of the burial on 30 March 1606 of one William Pory, Esquire, who may have been the father of John. William, the father, disposed of his land in Thompson, Norfolk, in 1590 and was not thereafter mentioned in local records. In fact, the entry concerning the christening of John and Mary Pory on 16 March 1572, is the last entry in the register of that parish concerning the family. John Pory possibly followed the example of his father in returning to the home of his ancestors at the end of his life.

∾ A LETTER OF LONDON NEWS

[John Pory to John Scudamore, 4 February 1632, Public Record Office, C115/M.35/391. John Scudamore, Baron Dromore and Viscount Scudamore of Sligo (1601–71), of Holme Lacy, Herefordshire, was the nephew of the wife of Sir Thomas Dale, governor of Virginia, 1611 and 1614 to 1616. In 1623 he was one of the adventurers in the Virginia Company. He had served in Parliament four times and afterwards was ambassador at Paris. At this particular time, however, he was living quietly at his country seat, grafting apple trees, planting orchards, and raising horses. During the civil war he fought for the king, afterwards suffering imprisonment and heavy fines at the hands of Parliament. When released he retired to engage in study and a program of aid to impoverished clergy.]

Right Honorable:
Since my last unto your lordship I understand that Doctor Freewin[57] having about a yeare agon erected an altar with a Canopy over it, in Magdalen Colledge chappell in Oxford where hee is president, hath nowe this winter caused a faire Crucifixe to be painted above the same altar with the pictures of the Virgin Mary and Mary Magdalen sitting weeping at the foot thereof, as the use is at Rome, Madrid, Brussells, or any other place where the Roman Catholique religion most prevaileth. Likewise in the East chancell-window of St. Gregories church newly repaired,[58] which leaneth upon the Southwest corner of Paules one Mr Hart a Proctor hath caused another Cruci-

57. Accepted Frewen (1588–1664) was president of Magdalene College from 1626 to 1643; afterwards he became bishop of Lichfield and Coventry. He became archbishop of York in 1660 and served until his death.
58. Inigo Jones as surveyor of the king's works made a report on the repairs to St. Gregory's on 14 June 1631, and he was especially cautioned several times to see that no damage resulted to St. Paul's by this work.

fixe to be painted, whereat some of the Parishe doe repine, but knowe not yet how to mende themselves. On Munday the lord high Constables Court for tryall of the two Scottishmen was a thirde time adjourned untill Munday next: for I heare their lordships at the Counsell board cannot yet agree, whether the busines shall ende in a combat, or bee referred to the Common lawe. Upon Wedensday one Mr Carrier a Minister was censured in the Starr chamber at £500 fine, and imprisonment during the kinges pleasure, and referred over to the high Commission for Royots, oppressions, extorsions, Champerties, &ct and for prophane speaking, so that they haste but a payer of shires between our Religion and Popery, and that it skill'd not which of the twoe a man professed. That whether there were a Purgatory or noe was a disputable question and a man might holde the affirmative as safely as the negative. That so the Clergy might fetche their meanes and maintenance out of the Layty, it made no matter if the Layty went to the Divell. Upon which point my lord Bishop of Winchester said among other thinges, that one Doctor Carrier[59] (who afterward turned Papist, and fled beyond sea) preaching in the chappell before King James some pointes of Popery, after the sermon ended a reverend Judge then present said to his lordship If you have any letters to sende to Rome here is a Carrier going that waye. But (said his lordship) this second Carrier will not perhaps goe to Rome, but will goe by Rome to the Divell. Also his lordship wish't that the old prayer of K. Ed. the 6th his time might be inserted againe into the Litany, to this or the like effect From the Tyranny of the Pope, and from his Idolatry and Superstition: good lord deliver us. Three of the lordes fined him at £2000. but the major part stood for £500. and therefore he escaped so good cheap. Some thinges well chardg'd against him in the bill were but weakly proov'd, and other thinges well proov'd were but weakly charg'd, which was the chief cause why his punishment was so light. Yesterday Sir Richard Grenvill[60] of the west was in the same court censured at £8000. (£4000 fine to the king, and

59. I have been unable to identify the Mr. Carrier. The Dr. Carrier referred to by the bishop of Winchester, however, was Benjamin Carrier (1566–1614), graduate of Corpus Christi, Cambridge, 1587, who became university preacher in 1597. He was also chaplain to King James, prebend of Canterbury (1608), and fellow of Chelsea Hospital. After joining the Church of Rome he went to Liège, and apparently was in Paris at the time of his death.

60. Sir Richard Grenville (1600–58), baronet and grandson of the man of the same name who took Raleigh's colonists to Roanoke Island. His dispute with the Earl of Suffolk, brother of his wife's first husband, grew out of the refusal of the Earl to pay money due to Lady Grenville. For further details of this and of another suit in which Grenville was involved, see the sketch of him in the *Dictionary of National Biography*. In both cases fines fell heavily upon him.

£4000 damages to my lord of Suffolke) for calling his lordship a base lorde.[61] Within the compasse of this week also Mr Walter Steward[62] having mett with Sir Miles Fleetwood[63] Treasurer of the Court of Wardes at my lord Treasurers, said he was a briber and hee would proove him so, and would lay him flatt on his back as hee had done the Earle of Middlesexe;[64] yea more, that he was a base knave, and that hee went to twoe sermons on a Sunday, and that on Munday morning hee would sell his friend for twoe shillings. Of this affronte Sir Miles complaining to the lordes, their lordships enjoined Mr Steward to give him in their presence such satisfaction as they thought reasonable. Their lordships made my lord Thurles[65] of Irland also to doe the like satisfaction to Captaine Essex.[66] The occasion was this. This Captaine attending and accompanying my Lady of Essex in a boxe in the playhouse at the black fryers, the said lord coming upon the stage, stood before them and hindred their sight. Captain Essex told his lordship they had payd for their place as well as hee, and therfore intreated him not to deprive them of the benefitt of it. Whereupon the lord stood up yet higher and hindred more their sight. Then Capt. Essex with his hand putt him a little by. The lord then drewe his sword and ran full butt at him, though he missed him, and might have slaine the Countesse as well as him. Another quarrell was between the lord Edward Paulet brother to the Marques of Winchester and Mr Frederick Cornwal-

61. Theophilus Howard, second Earl of Suffolk (1584–1640), was the son of Thomas Howard, Duke of Suffolk, by his second wife whom he married "in or before 1583," as *The Complete Peerage* (London, 1953), 12:465 expresses it. Their son was born 13 August 1584. Grenville may have known the precise date of the marriage and that the bride was pregnant at the time.

62. Perhaps the one of this name who was the third son of Walter Steward, Baron Blantyre. The younger Walter Steward was created M.A. at Cambridge in 1615 on the king's visit and admitted at Gray's Inn, 1620. He afterwards sat in Parliament and was also a doctor of medicine. He took refuge in France after 1649. One Wat Steward went on 28 September 1632 to take a message to Ambassador Weston at Turin.

63. Sir Miles Fleetwood (d. 1641), father of several distinguished sons, served in Parliament, 1614–28. He had been knighted at Dublin Castle in 1602 by Charles Blount, Lord Mountjoy, lord deputy of Ireland.

64. Lionel Cranfield, Earl of Middlesex (1575–1645), may have been called upon by Steward to account for certain arrearages while he held office under the Crown. For an additional reference to this subject see the letter of 28 April 1632.

65. James Butler, Lord Thurles (1610–88), who was created Duke of Ormond in 1682. When he was nine his father drowned at sea, and he became a royal ward, being educated by Archbishop Abbot at Lambeth. Pory's report suggests that he was an impetuous youth, but he later had a distinguished career.

66. Probably Charles Essex who had been "bred up a page" under the Earl of Essex. He may well have accompanied the Countess of Essex to the theatre. Essex, a colonel at the time, was killed at the Battle of Edgehill in 1642.

leis of the Court.[67] Hee kickt Mr Cornwalleis out of a report or Jelousy, he should have said, his lordship had the poxe. Their lordships at the bourd enjoining his lordship to doe some satisfaction to Mr Cornwalleis, and he refusing, hee was sent to the Marshallseyes. Mr Walter Long[68] being redelivered by the sheriff back into the Tower meeting with the Lieutenant tolde him: I am come back with my head on my shoulders. What mean you by that, said Mr Lieutenant. I tell you this (quoth Mr Long) because the last man whom the sheriff carried hence was brought hither again head lesse. The Barons of the Exchequer have given the same Mr Long respitt till next Wedensday to bring in his answere to Sir Robert Heaths bill, which if he doe not they will then take it pro confesso, and send for the Extents upon his lande. One that dwelles in the Tower tolde me yesterday, that Sir John Elyot, when he was remooved out of the kinges lodging was putt to a place called Coleharbour, being part of the great square tower, and one of the vilest lodgings in all the house. Where when his eyes were almost smoak'd out, praying the Lieutenant he might have a lodging where he might live at least, Mr Lieutenant borrowed the house of my lord Vere Master of the Ordinance, which next unto the privy lodginges is the best in all the Tower, and standes upon the highest ground. Sir John Heydon,[69] Lieutenant of the Ordinance there, hath called all the officers that are under him to an account, what hath bene issued, of Ordinance, munitions, &ct, out of the kinges stores, since the yeare 1620. And it is like to cost somebody the setting on. He hath also a project inhande to have armes of all kindes to be made here in England, sufficient for the use of the kingdome, that we may not be beholding to strangers for them. And to finde out where any man that should have armes, doe want them, hee is about to obtaine of his Majesty that a generall muster may be made throughout all England & Wales in one & the same daye; so that none of the

67. The minutes of the council for 3 February by Secretary Coke show, "Lord Edward Pawlett and Sir Frederick Cornwallis committed." Cornwallis was the son of Sir William Cornwallis and his second wife, Jane Mewtas. He was an ancestor of Lord Charles Cornwallis who fought in the American Revolution.

68. Long had been confined in the Tower since 1629 for his "seditious practices and crimes of a high nature" as a member of Parliament when he supported Sir John Eliot. His wife died while he was confined and his children were left "motherless, fatherless, and friendless." During the civil war he was an outspoken partisan of Parliament. He may be the same Walter Long who represented Bath in Parliament in 1643.

69. Sir John Heydon (d. 1653) later served as lieutenant general of the ordnance to Charles I during the civil war.

divers parishes may lend or borrow armes. Sir Francis Nethersall[70] Secretary to the Queen of Bohemia is newly returned from her, saying, he thinkes veryly ere this, that both kinges are mett, the king of Bohemia having sett forth from the Hagh on Tuesday was fortnight. At his departure the states presented him £15000. in money, and the Prince of Orange with £2000. and eight goodly coach-horses. And the States tolde him, that whatsoever his brother of Great Britain would doe for him, they would doe as muche. If he would send him 500. men into the Palatinat, they would send 500. also: and if he would send ten thousand, they would send as many. Besides the people of Holland shewed more affection toward him at his departure, then ever they did before, honouring him with accla-mations, farewells, and benedictions, as if he had bene their naturall Prince. Three things of late have bene muche agitated here in mens mouths. First the relief of Magdenburg by Count Papenheim. Sec-ondly that the king of Sweden should be taken prisoner. And 3dly that the French king & hee should be fallen out. As touching the first, I am tolde out of letters from Leipsig and from Hamburgh, that Papenheim being too strong for Bannier the kinges General which layd siedge to the Towne, Bannier suffred him to enter it without any resistance. (Where some say, he burnt the Cathedrall church and all the houses remaining, and blewe up some of the chief Bulwarkes, and so brought all the Emperors garrison & their baggage out of the towne: others that he onely took out the sick which he carried away in carts & waggons and left strong men in their places.) But all agree that Oxenstierne great Chancelour of Sweden coming luckly that way with 2000. brave horse did adde such strength & countenance to the kinges army, as when Papen-heim was come clear out of the towne, they charg'd him on the reare, routed all his troupes, in so much as with 15. horse he was forced to flee into Wolfenbuttle. That the king of Sweden was taken prisoner is a fable; the morall wherof is this. When hee went to visit and welcome his Queen, shee embraced him with this Salutation: Sir, nowe you are my prisoner nowe. And for the French king, I heard Sir D. A. late Agent in the lowe countries say, it was very dangerous for the French king at this time be at Jarres with the king of Sweden, not onely because Monsieur (who aspires at his Crowne) is nowe regaled like a king in Brussells with 800. men in his traine;

70. Sir Francis Nethersole (1587–1659), formerly a tutor at Trinity College, Cambridge, had also once been secretary to James Hay, Viscount Doncaster, prior to entering the service of the Electress Elizabeth in 1620.

but also for that the Emperor laboureth now might and maine with the king of Sweden for a peace, suche as might be honorable to him, and safe for the German Protestants his friends. So that in case the French king might have the courage and power to impeach any of that kinges designes, he might then abandon him, and leave him to the mercie of the house of Austria. Your lordships most humble servant

Appendix

List of Letters and Other Minor Writings on Microfiche

17 Nov 1600	London	Sir Robert Cecil, 1
After 17 Nov 1600	[Cambridge?]	Custodian, Gonville and Caius College, 2
7 Jan 1606	[London]	Sir Robert Cotton, 3
Summer 1606	[London]	[Sir Robert Cotton], 5
12 Aug 1606	[London]	Sir Robert Cotton, 7
3 Jan 1610	[London]	Dudley Carleton, 11
17 Jul 1610	[London]	Sir Ralph Winwood, 13
2 Feb 1612	Paris	Sir Robert Cotton, 16
30 Jun 1612	Paris	Sir Robert Cotton, 18
3 Oct 1612	The Hague	[Sir Dudley Carleton], 20
9 Oct 1612	Brussels	[Sir Dudley Carleton], 20
19 Mar 1613	Paris	Sir Dudley Carleton, 22
16 Jul 1613	Turin	Sir Thomas Edmondes, 24
18 Dec 1614	Constantinople	Sir Dudley Carleton, 26
29 Apr 1616	Constantinople	Sir Dudley Carleton, 29
Sep 1616	Constantinople	Sir Dudley Carleton, 31
20 Oct 1616	Constantinople	Sir Dudley Carleton, 33
8 Nov 1617	London	Sir Dudley Carleton, 34
30 Aug 1618	Margate	Sir Dudley Carleton, 36
5 Sep 1618	London	Sir Dudley Carleton, 37
25 Oct 1618	London	Sir Dudley Carleton, 38
31 Oct 1618	London	Sir Dudley Carleton, 42
7 Nov 1618	London	Sir Dudley Carleton, 45
14 Nov 1618	London	Sir Dudley Carleton, 48
28 Nov 1618	London	Sir Dudley Carleton, 50
Winter 1619	Jamestown	[Sir Dudley Carleton], 52
30 Sep 1619	Jamestown	Sir Dudley Carleton, 72
13 Jan 1620	Jamestown	Sir Edwin Sandys, 75
14 Jan 1620	Jamestown	Sir Edwin Sandys, 79
16 Jan 1620	Jamestown	Sir Edwin Sandys, 80
12 Jun 1620	Jamestown	Sir Edwin Sandys, 83
9 May 1621	Jamestown	Sir Edwin Sandys, 87

After 18 Nov 1621	Jamestown	[Earl of Southampton?], 88
28 Aug 1622	[On board ship?]	William Bradford, 91
Late summer 1622	[Monhegan]	[Sir Francis Wyatt], 92
After 13 Jan 1623	Angra, Azores	Earl of Southampton, 95
3 Jun 1625	[London]	The Rev. Joseph Mead, 99
8 Oct 1625	Cambridge	The Rev. Joseph Mead to Sir Martin Stuteville quoting Pory, 101
28 Apr 1626	London	The Rev. Joseph Mead, 104
5 Jul 1626	London	The Rev. Joseph Mead, 104
11 Aug 1626	London	The Rev. Joseph Mead, 108
17 Aug 1626	London	The Rev. Joseph Mead, 111
2 Sep 1626	London	The Rev. Joseph Mead, 113
23 Nov 1626	[London]	The Rev. Joseph Mead, 115
26 Nov 1626	London	The Rev. Joseph Mead, 116
2 Mar 1627	London	The Rev. Joseph Mead, 118
22 Jun 1627	London	The Rev. Joseph Mead, 119
2 Nov 1627	[London]	The Rev. Joseph Mead, 120
Before 13 Apr 1628	[London]	The Rev. Joseph Mead, 121
28 Apr 1628	[London]	[Enclosure to the Rev. Joseph Mead], 122
21 Jun 1628	[London]	[The Rev. Joseph Mead], 124
26 Jun 1628	[London]	[The Rev. Joseph Mead], 125
Before 20 Sep 1628	[London]	The Rev. Joseph Mead, 127
14 Nov 1628	London	The Rev. Joseph Mead, 128
21 Nov 1628	London	The Rev. Joseph Mead, 131
28 Nov 1628	London	The Rev. Joseph Mead, 133
5 Dec 1628	London	The Rev. Joseph Mead, 136
12 Dec 1628	London	The Rev. Joseph Mead, 139
19 Dec 1628	London	The Rev. Joseph Mead, 141
9 Apr 1629	London	The Rev. Joseph Mead, 144
12 Feb 1630	London	The Rev. Joseph Mead, 145
30 Oct 1630	London	[The Rev. Joseph Mead], 149
27 Nov 1630	London	[The Rev. Joseph Mead], 150
13 Jan 1631	London	Sir Thomas Puckering, 151
21 Apr 1631	London	Sir Thomas Puckering, 154
12 May 1631	London	Sir Thomas Puckering, 159
16 Jun 1631	London	Sir Thomas Puckering, 163
8 Sep 1631	London	Sir Thomas Puckering, 167
22 Sep 1631	London	Sir Thomas Puckering 170
17 Nov 1631	London	Sir Thomas Puckering, 174

1 Dec 1631	London	Sir Thomas Puckering, 179
4 Dec 1631	London	John, Viscount Scudamore, 181
12 Dec 1631	London	John, Viscount Scudamore, 183
14 Dec 1631	London	Sir Thomas Puckering, 186
17 Dec 1631	London	John, Viscount Scudamore, 189
24 Dec 1631	London	John, Viscount Scudamore, 190
31 Dec 1631	London	John, Viscount Scudamore, 193
12 Jan 1632	London	Sir Thomas Puckering, 196
12 Jan 1632	London	John, Viscount Scudamore, 199
26 Jan 1632	London	Sir Thomas Puckering, 202
4 Feb 1632	London	John, Viscount Scudamore, 205
11 Feb 1632	London	John, Viscount Scudamore, 209
18 Feb 1632	London	John, Viscount Scudamore, 213
23 Feb 1632	London	Sir Thomas Puckering, 215
25 Feb 1632	London	John, Viscount Scudamore, 219
3 Mar 1632	London	John, Viscount Scudamore, 223
17 Mar 1632	London	John, Viscount Scudamore, 226
24 Mar 1632	London	John, Viscount Scudamore, 231
31 Mar 1632	London	John, Viscount Scudamore, 236
7 Apr 1632	London	John, Viscount Scudamore, 241
14 Apr 1632	London	John, Viscount Scudamore, 245
21 Apr 1632	London	John, Viscount Scudamore, 249
28 Apr 1632	London	John, Viscount Scudamore, 253
5 May 1632	London	John, Viscount Scudamore, 257
12 May 1632	London	John, Viscount Scudamore, 260

18 May 1632	London	John, Viscount Scudamore, 265
26 May 1632	London	John, Viscount Scudamore, 268
9 Jun 1632	London	John, Viscount Scudamore, 272
16 Jun 1632	London	John, Viscount Scudamore, 276
23 Jun 1632	London	John, Viscount Scudamore, 279
29 Jun 1632	London	John, Viscount Scudamore, 283
1 Sep 1632	London	John, Viscount Scudamore, 286
8 Sep 1632	London	John, Viscount Scudamore, 288
15 Sep 1632	London	John, Viscount Scudamore, 292
20 Sep 1632	London	Sir Thomas Puckering, 294
22 Sep 1632	London	John, Viscount Scudamore, 297
29 Sep 1632	London	John, Viscount Scudamore, 300
6 Oct 1632	London	John, Viscount Scudamore, 303
13 Oct 1632	London	John, Viscount Scudamore, 305
20 Oct 1632	London	John, Viscount Scudamore, 308
25 Oct 1632	London	Robert Greville, Baron Brooke, 311
27 Oct 1632	London	John, Viscount Scudamore, 314
1 Nov 1632	London	Sir Thomas Lucy, 317
3 Nov 1632	London	John, Viscount Scudamore, 320
10 Nov 1632	London	John, Viscount Scudamore, 323
15 Nov 1632	London	Robert Greville, Baron Brooke, 326
17 Nov 1632	London	John, Viscount Scudamore, 329
24 Nov 1632	London	John, Viscount Scudamore, 332

1 Dec 1632	London	John, Viscount Scudamore, 334
6 Dec 1632	London	Robert Greville, Baron Brooke, 337
8 Dec 1632	London	John, Viscount Scudamore, 339
13 Dec 1632	London	Robert Greville, Baron Brooke, 342
15 Dec 1632	London	John, Viscount Scudamore, 345
3 Jan 1633	London	Sir Thomas Puckering, 346
24 Jan 1633	London	Sir Thomas Puckering, 348

D. ROBERTUS COTTONUS BRUCEUS,
Eques Auratus et Baronettus,
Bibliothecæ COTTONIANÆ. *Fundator .*

Courtesy British Library

Sir Robert Cotton, to whom Pory wrote between 1606 and 1612.

Sir Dudley Carleton, Pory's long-time friend and employer.

The Right Honourable
Sr RALPH WINWOOD Kn.^t
Principall Secretary of State and Privy
Councellour to his Majesty King IAMES the First.

Ætatis suæ XIIX.

M. a Miereveldt pinxit A.° 1613.   *Geo. Vertue Sculpsit 1725.*

Sir Ralph Winwood, secretary of state, for whom Pory worked briefly at Whitehall in 1617.

THE RIGHT HON. SIR THOMAS EDMONDS, KNT.

Courtesy British Library

Sir Thomas Edmondes, British ambassador in Paris, to whom Pory wrote in 1613 from Turin.

*Victor Amadeus I, Prince of Piedmont, who engaged Pory in lengthy
conversation at Millefleur, near Turin, in July 1613.*

Enlargement of the wax seal on Pory's letter of 16 July 1613, from Turin, to Sir Thomas Edmondes.

Courtesy The Public Record Office

Pory's letter to Sir Dudley Carleton written from Constantinople, September 1616.

upon his head 3. or 4. times together, and sayde he
would leaue it as a monumente of honour to his poste=
=rity. Besides he saide, he made no doubte, but to
get it printed euen in Italy it selfe, mary therin
he would could consulte w.th his Ma.ties Ambassadger
at Venice. It may be that some other of greater
sufficiency then my selfe hath already better perfor=
=med it then my selfe haue done. If it be so, all
the better. But had I through sloathe or cowardice
refused such a labour, wherein I was to publishe
his Ma.ties renowne in these remote & barbarous parts,
I had merited eternal disgrace, & rendered my selfe
unworthy to haue bene esteemed his Ma.ties subject.
Yet so farr as I knowe I aroue, I shall not wante to grace
any serious attempte of myne, so farr forth as you shall
see juste cause; and for the sufficiency of my perfor=
=mance in this, the Bayle by their resident in Eng=
=lande will giue ample testimony to his Ma.tie And
if euer god lende me to Padoa, I haue another attempt
there, w.ch (his diuine Ma.tie giuing me life and healthe)
as in a maner secure my selfe, will make up my
fortunes, and will make so (that w.ch I shall thinke the
greatest happines in this worlde) the payment of my
debts. What joye I can haue in staying here after my
lordes departure, in these times of dangers oppressions
and flatteries, I do not see. Yet if I can discouer
any hope of honour or proffite, my fortunes being

(as they are)

Pory's letter to Sir Dudley Carleton written from Constantinople,
September 1616.

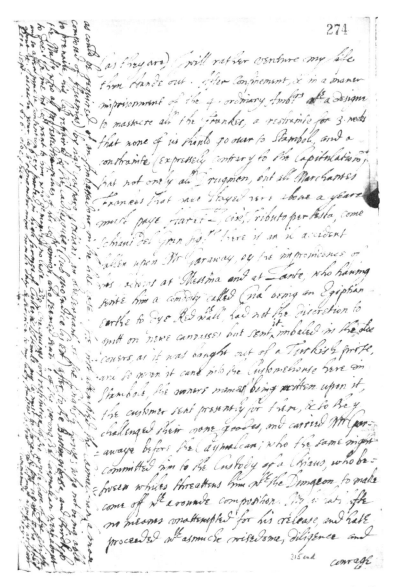

Courtesy The Public Record Office

Pory's letter to Sir Dudley Carleton written from Constantinople, September 1616.

Sir Edwyn Sandys, Second Son of Archbp. Sandys.
From an Original Picture.
Published Jan. 1st 1776.

Sir Edwin Sandys, treasurer of the Virginia Company, to whom Pory wrote in 1620 and 1621.

Henry Wriothesley, Earl of Southampton, *treasurer of the Virginia Company, to whom Pory wrote in 1621 and 1623.*

Robert Rich, second Earl of Warwick

King Charles I, whose reign covered the years 1625–49, was often mentioned by Pory in his correspondence.

Tomb of Sir Thomas Puckering (d. 1636), Warwick. Pory corresponded with Puckering from 1631 until 1633.

John, first Viscount Scudamore of Sligo

Courtesy His Grace, the Earl of Warwick

Robert Greville, Baron Brooke, to whom Pory wrote in 1632.

Index to the Biography ∿

Paramore, John: nominated as secretary for Virginia, 99
Parham, Sir Edward, 71
Paris, 37–39, 43, 58, 126
Parker, Matthew, Archbishop of Canterbury, 4
Parliament, 21, 25–30, 32, 56, 58, 60, 63, 65, 68, 80, 82, 87, 89, 92, 110n, 126, 128n. *See also* House of Commons
Patents: to be interpreted against the crown, 68
Paul IV, Pope, 15
Paul V, Pope, 41n
Paulet, Lord Edward, 128, 129n
Paulet, John. *See* Winchester, Marquis of
Pearl hatband: worn in Jamestown, 108
Pera, 42, 47. *See also* Constantinople
Percy, George, 24
Percy, Henry, 70
Perron, Cardinal. *See* DuPerron, Cardinal Jacques Davy
Persia, King of, 72
Persian Gulf, 72
Persian manuscript: presented to Oxford by Pory, 44
Phelips, Sir Edward, 25
Philip IV, King of Spain, 105
Pierse, Thomas, 88, 93
Piersey, Abraham, 113, 115, 119, 121
Pigafetta, Philippo, 12
Pilgrims, 87, 103
Pindar, Paul, 9, 42, 43, 45, 55, 57, 62
Pine trees: in Virginia, 83; in North Carolina area, 100–101
Pirates and piracy, 34, 36, 105
Plantations: in Virginia, 113, 114
Playhouse (theatre), 128
Pliny, 54
Plymouth, Devonshire, 77
Plymouth, Massachusetts, 103, 105
Poore, Richard, 4
Pope, 127. *See also* Leo X; Paul IV; Paul V
Porey, William (of Sutton St. Edmunds), 4n
Porie, Francis, 6n
Pory, Anne, 3, 100n
Pory, Sir John (fl. 1507), 4
Pory, John (1503–70), 4, 8
Pory, John (fl. 1570), 4n
Pory, John (1572–1636), birth and christening, 2, 3, 126; family arms, 5, 8; at Gonville and Caius College, 6;

receives degree from Oxford, 6; initials carved in choir stall, 7; instructor in Greek, 9; studies with Hakluyt and translates book on Africa, 12, 13, 15, 16, 46; words used by, 18; serves in Parliament, 26–30, 32; attends masque, 31–32; travel, 32; in Ireland, 34–36; in Paris, 37–41, 43; in Padua and Turin, 41; observes and reports disputation between Featly and Smith, 38–41; in Constantinople, 42–44; presents books to University of Oxford, 44; at The Hague, 48; as newsletter writer, 51, 53–59; sources of information, 56–57; personal characteristics, 59, 60, 62; trouble with drink, 59, 63n, 74; illness, 61, 107; financial problems, 62; secretary in Virginia, 74–83 passim, 107; interest in iron mine, 81–82; salt making, 82, 97; reports on conditions in Virginia, 82–84, 106–9; speaker of first legislature in America, 30, 84–96; travels to Eastern Shore, Chesapeake Bay, and Potomac River, 96–98; travels to Chowan River, 96–97, 100; visits New England, 103–5; shipwrecked in the Azores, 105; compiles Indian dictionary, 105; commissioner in Virginia, 113–23; final years, 123–26
Pory, John (d. 1681), 124n
Pory, Mrs. Margaret, 7
Pory, Mary (b. 1572), 3
Pory, Peter, 3n, 4n, 24
Pory, Robert, 4n, 24
Pory, the Rev. Dr. Robert, 5
Pory, William, 3, 4n, 7, 126
Porye, Richard, 6n
Post fines, 68
Potatoes, 98
Potomac River, 98, 99
Pottes, not to serve on Virginia Commission, 122
Pountis, John, 118
Powell, Nathaniel, 77, 87, 100
Powis, Lord (William Herbert), 58
Precedents, 66
Prefines, 68
Prerogatives, 68
Prince of Wales (Charles I), 105. *See also* Henry Frederick
Privy Council, 14, 49, 76, 111–14, 116–18, 120, 121
Progresses, 57
Puckering, Sir Thomas, 55, 56, 123

Virginia Land Office, 81
Virginia's God be Thanked, by Copland, 100

W
Wake, Isaac, 50
Wales, 129
Warde, Captain John, 87, 88
Wards, Master of the, 14, 67. *See also* Court of Wards
Ware Park, Hertfordshire, 43, 47
Warner, Walter, 24
Warwick, Earl of. *See* Rich, Sir Robert
Waterhouse, Edward, 101
Waterhouse, Thomas: nominated as secretary for Virginia, 99
Watling Street, London, 56
Watton, Curate Thomas, 124
Waymouth, Southcott, 33, 34n
Weather: in Virginia, 107
Webster, John, 17
Welshmen, 66
Wentworth: punished for speaking against the king of France, 37
Wentworth, Sir Thomas, Earl of Strafford, 123, 124
West, Francis, 115
West, Sir Thomas, 74
West Indies, 106, 109n
Weston, Jerome, Earl of Portland, 128n
Wetheringsett, Suffolk, 9, 10
Wheat, 4, 107
White Devil, by John Webster, 17
Whitehall, London, 17, 43, 57, 69, 71n, 72
Wilton, Wiltshire: Pory visits, 120n
Winchester, Bishop of. *See* Neile, Richard
Winchester, Marquis of (John Paulet), 128
Winwood, Sir Ralph, 9, 26, 28, 43, 55, 57, 63, 65
Wolfenbuttle, Germany, 130
Wood Street, London, 56, 109n
Worcester, Earl of. *See* Somerset, Edward
Words: obsolete and new, used by Pory, 18–19
Wotton, Sir Henry, 9, 43
Wriothesley, Henry, Earl of Southampton, 74, 102, 103, 105, 110, 118
Wyatt, Sir Francis, 99, 115. *See also* Governor of Virginia
Wyatt, Lady Margaret, 119

Y
Yeardley, Sir George, 5, 56, 74–81, 83, 84, 86, 90, 92, 94, 97, 99, 109, 115, 124n. *See also* Governor of Virginia
Yeardley, Ralph, 56, 109
Yeardley, Temperance Flowerdew, 5, 74, 123n
Yelverton, Sir Henry, 70

Z
Zanzibar, 15

Index to the Microfiche ~~

285, 286, 289, 301, 304; gaudy procession at, 167; letters from, 172, 233, 238, 276, 282, 285, 290, 295, 298, 338; post from, 179, 186, 213, 250, 251, 306, 319, 333; King of Spain entertained at, 217; flatbottom boats from, 224, 287, 289; flood near, 277–78, 282, 285, 290; citizens fortify, 299

Antwerp, pensioner of, 350

Antwerp, Corantos, 314, 318

Apostles, eleven, 14

Apothecaries, Society of, 75

Apparel. *See* Dress

"Appeal to Caesar" (*Appello Caesarean: A Just Appeale From Two Unjust Informers*), by Richard Montagu, 134, 135, 140

Aquavitae, 137

Aragon, Spain, 267

Archduchess. *See* Isabella Clara Eugenia

Arenstat: King of Sweden at, 347

Argall, Captain Samuel, 56, 68, 69, 72, 75–77, 80, 92, 93, 101, 103, 104

Argall Towne (Paspahegh), Virginia, 68, 69

Argall's Gift, Virginia, 53

Aristotle, quoted, 271

Armada, 254

Arminianism, 134, 140, 141

Arminians, 126, 134

Arminius, Jacobus, 141, 228

Arms and ammunition, 171, 207. *See also* Carbine; Guns; Powder; Shot

Arnheim, Netherlands, 203, 204, 279, 328, 331

Arnauld, Pere Antoine, 327, 331

Arras, Turkey, 301

Arschot, Duke of, 278, 350

Art collection, 144

Articles of Peace, 152, 162

Articles of Religion, 134, 135

Artois, France, 217, 221, 293, 299, 301

Arundel, Earl of. *See* Howard, Thomas

Arundel, Lady. *See* Talbot, Althea

Arundel House, 144

Ashburnham, Mrs., 118

Ashburnham, Sir John, 192, 193

Ashmolean Museum, Oxford, 320

Assacomoco (Indian town in Virginia), 89

Assembly in Scotland, 112

Assenburgh (Assen), Netherlands, 175

Assurance, 140

Astley (Ashley), Sir Jacob, 238–40, 284

Astley, Sir John, 4

Aston, Walter, Baron Aston of Forfar, 213–16, 218, 219

Astrologer, 267

Astronomers, 51

Attainder, 13, 16

Attorney general. *See* Heath, Sir Robert; Noye, William

Attorneys, 165

Attoughcomoco, Virginia, 89

Audley, Sir Ferdinando. *See* Touchet, Ferdinando, Lord Audley

Augsburg, Germany, 244, 246, 250, 251, 255, 259, 263, 266, 274, 281, 284, 285, 321

Augustus, Duke, 239

Auigliana, Germany: captured, 150

l'Ausbespine, Charles de, Marquis de Chasteauneuf, 233, 236

Austria, 20, 21, 175, 180, 181, 201, 204, 211, 212, 255, 279, 313, 316, 319, 321, 325

Austria, Barons of, 270

Austria, House of, 173, 175, 176, 179, 182, 185, 190, 193, 197, 201, 208, 211, 214, 217, 222, 224, 229, 249, 253, 275, 312, 314, 346, 347

Auvergne, France, 162

Avignon, France, 195

d'Aylona, Marques, 301

Azores. *See* Angra do Heroísmo

Ayn in Henault, 302

B

Babel no Bethel, by Henry Burton, 145

Baccleuch, Earl of. *See* Scott, Walter

Bacon, Sir Francis, Baron Verulam, 46, 47, 155, 158

Baden, Marquis of: defeated, 348. *See also* Christopher, Marquis of Baden

Badger, Tom, 46, 48

Badgercraft, Mr., 115

Badgers, 334, 337

Baffin, William, 50

Bagg, Sir James, 210, 212, 215, 274

Bahia (des Todos Santos), Brazil, 156, 159, 161, 163

Bainards Castle, 340

Bainton, Sir Edmund, 258

Baize (bayes) cloth, 143

Baker, Iris, 192

Balcanqual, Dr. Walter, 193, 196

Baldwin, William, 301, 302

Balfore, Colonel, 276

Balloon (Baloun, Boloen), 281, 283, 285

Balthazar de Simmeren, Jean, Don, Governor of Prague, 179
Baltic Sea, 119, 164
Baltimore, Lord. *See* Calvert, George
Balzac, Jean Louis Guez de, 215
Bamberg, Bishop of, 211
Bamberg, Germany, 176, 218, 222, 234, 238, 243, 309
Banbury, Earl of. *See* Knollys, William
Baner, Johan, 207, 217, 221, 247, 248, 255, 299, 344
Banquet, 7, 20, 34
Banqueting House, 167, 197, 199
Barbados, 178, 237, 286
Barbary, 119, 120, 155. *See also* Sydan, Muley; Hamet, Muley
Barbary, Sultan of. *See* Muley Hamet
Barberini, Maffeo, Pope Urban VIII, 196. *See also* Popes
Barbougon, Prince of, 167
Barcelona, 267
Bargrove, Captain John, 63
Barillon, President, 162
Barker, Christopher, 264
Barker, Robert, 261, 264
Barley, 250
Barnardiston, Sir Nathanial, 118
Barnham, Sir Francis, 156, 159
Barnsted Down, 294, 298
Barrell, Gilbert, 146
Barrett, Edward, Lord of Newburgh, 142, 144
Barriers, 3
Barrow, Sir John, 120
Bass (fish), 96
Bassompierre, Francis de, 114, 115
Bassond, John, 292
Bastille, 17, 115, 316
Bath, Countess of. *See* St. John, Dorothy
Bath, Earl of. *See* Bourchier, Edward
Bath, Somersetshire, 145, 294
Bauditz, Colonel, 164; General, 288, 303, 321, 325, 333, 348
Bautzen (Bauditzon), Germany, 259, 262, 267, 270
Bavaria, 177, 181, 244–46, 254, 255, 259, 262, 263, 266, 267, 270, 281, 284, 290, 296, 309, 316, 319, 321, 324, 325
Bavaria, Duke of, 171, 198, 210, 212, 221, 250, 251, 255, 256, 259, 266, 274, 275, 285, 293, 296, 324, 344
Bavarians, 256
Bayonne, France, 324, 328
Bazan, Alvaro de, second Marquis of

Santa Cruz, 149, 172, 233, 236, 278, 299, 301
Beare, Sydney, 312, 315
Beare, 7
Beauchamp, Lord. *See* Seymour, Edward
Beauclerc, Monsieur: charged with rape and murder, 309
Beaumont, Francis, 294
Beaumont, Mary, Countess of Buckingham, 109, 111, 135, 137, 154, 249, 252, 253, 279
Beaver, 151, 217, 220, 243; hat, 74; skins, 89
Bedford, Countess of. *See* Harington, Lucy
Bedford, Earl of. *See* Russell, Edward; Russell, Francis
Bee sting, 164
Beecher, Sir William, 40, 41, 236, 239, 241
Beer, 112
Belasyse, Henry, 232, 235
Belasyse, Sir Thomas, Baron Fauconberg, 165, 166, 232, 235
Bell (pupil of Joseph Mead), 103
Bellasset, Henry. *See* Belasyse, Henry
Bellegarde, Grand Duc de, 162
Belt. *See* Little Belt
Benet College, Cambridge, 226, 241, 242
Benfield, Alsatia, 322, 325, 332
Benjamin (benzoin), 5
Bergen op Zoom, Netherlands, 100, 172
Berkeley, Lady, 4
Berkeley, Sir Robert, 306, 307
Bermuda Islands (Somer Islands), 83, 87, 95. *See also* Somers Island Company
Bermuda Islands Company, 117. *See also* Somers Island Company
Berrington (a merchant), 338
Berry, France, 162
Bertie, Peregrine, Lord Willoughby, 4, 113, 117
Bertie, Robert, Baron Willoughby and Earl of Lindsey, 110, 128–30, 177, 268, 271; Lord Chamberlain, 226, 268, 273, 276, 347
Beziers, France, 293, 316
Bible, 38, 89, 200, 261, 264
Bilbao, Spain, 251
Bins: taken, 325
Biscay, Spain, 180, 182, 322, 327, 330; Bay of, 121, 130, 320

Brooke, Samuel, 173, 174
Browne (a messenger), 338
Browning, Giles, 166
Bruges, Belgium, 253
Bruncard, Sir William, 128
Brunswick, 21, 251, 254, 260
Brunswick, Duke of, 21, 254
Brussels, 20, 129, 171, 185, 195, 198, 204, 205, 208, 210, 211, 233, 270, 277, 278, 287–90, 292, 296, 299, 301, 304, 312, 315, 317, 319, 323, 333, 342, 350, 351
Buccleuch, Duke of. See Montagu-Douglas-Scott, Walter John
Bucke, Richard (minister), 53
Buckingham, Countess of. See Beaumont, Mary
Buckingham, Duchess of. See Manners, Katherine
Buckingham, Duke of. See Villiers, George
Buckingham, England, 158
Budweitz, Bohemia, 180, 181, 198
Bull, Papal: against the King of Sweden, 177, 239
Bulldogs, 48
Burghley, Baron. See Cecil, Thomas
Burgo Maria, Italy, 139, 141
Burgundy, Duke of, 224
Burgundy, France, 153, 281
Burial. See Funerals
Burick, Germany, 186
Burlamachi, Philip, 118, 119, 143, 144, 151, 169, 216, 220, 233, 236, 321, 335, 337, 338, 347
Burton, Henry, 144, 145
Busher, Leonard, 36, 37
Bushire (Jasques), Iran, 39, 41
Busse (place), 287, 288, 328
Busse (ship), 305, 323, 327, 330, 332
Butler, Elizabeth: marries Richard Preston, 50
Butler, James, Earl of Ormond and Ossory and Lord Thurles, 138, 139, 206, 209
Butler, Walter, eleventh Earl of Ormond, 48, 50, 138, 139
Butter, 143
Butter, Nathaniel, 190, 193, 212, 272, 309–12, 314, 318; shop of, 276
Button, Sir Thomas, 151, 153
Butts, Dr. Henry, vice chancellor of Cambridge University, 223, 226, 241, 242, 244
Buxtehude, Germany, 225

C

Cadiz, 104, 240, 242, 254
Cadiz Expedition, 1625, 140
Caesar, Julius, 288, 302
Caius College, Cambridge. See Gonville and Caius College
Calais, 143, 147, 151, 159, 179, 181, 197, 225, 252, 254, 258, 259, 263, 266, 270, 272, 278, 280, 289, 292, 296, 299, 322
Calendar. See Julian calendar
Calico, 142
Calvert, George, Lord Baltimore, 145, 148, 249, 253
Calvin, John, 141, 347
Calvinists, 262, 324
Cambodia (Camboia), 5, 6
Cambray, France, 79, 171, 278, 290, 299
Cambridge, 16, 152, 216, 219, 223, 225–27, 232, 241, 242, 250, 258, 279, 282, 292, 294, 299, 306
Cambridgeshire, 287
Camden, Viscount. See Noel, Edward
Camerarius, Ludwig, 212
Campbell, Archibald, Earl of Argile, 265, 267
Canada, 86, 93, 97, 99, 151, 220, 242; fishing in, 83. See also Quebec
Candale, Monsieur de: breaks both legs, 23
Candle, 131, 132
Candlemas, 199
Cannibals. See Man-eaters
Canoes, 89; not to be taken in Virginia, 66
Canterbury, 38, 101, 109
Canterbury, Archbishop of. See Abbot, George
Capawacke Indians, 98
Capawacke Island, Massachusetts, 98
Cape Anna, Massachusetts, 93, 95
Cape Charles, Virginia, 87, 93
Cape Cod, 92, 95, 99
Cape Henry, Virginia, 93
Cape Merchant, 59, 63, 64, 71. See also Magazine
Capell, Sir Arthur, 245, 248
Capital punishment. See Woman
Capp, William, 52, 56
Captains, nine: Denbigh finds fault with, 143
Capuchin Chapel, Somerset House, 294, 296, 297
Capuchins, 171

289, 291, 300, 304, 305, 311, 312, 313, 315, 317, 318, 320, 321, 335, 336, 337, 339, 341, 342, 343, 344, 349, 350; at Dover, 100; at Salisbury, 101; speech for Commons, 122, 125; commands concerning Felton, 129, 136; reaction to war in Germany, 177; equestrian statue by Le Sueur, 181; quoted by Pory, 190–91; as prince, 212, 214, 317, 336; accounts with Buckingham, 237; gives horses to King of Spain, 242; annual pension for ambergis, 250; league with King of Sweden, 257; guards against King of France, 258; to send ambassador to Sweden, 261; letters to Ferdinand II, 284; called "king of devils," 310; given petition on behalf of Sir John Eliot, 332

Charles II: as prince, 306, 317, 319, 321

Charles IV, Duke of Lorraine, 162, 177, 194, 196, 197, 201, 211, 224, 244, 270, 281

Charles V, 293

Charles (East India ship), 155

Charles City, Virginia, 52, 67

Charles Emmanuel I (1562–1630), Duke of Savoy, 26, 72, 75, 100, 118, 128, 139, 277, 283, 286

Charles Lewis (oldest son of Elizabeth of Bohemia and Frederick V), 335, 338, 340

Chasteauneuf, Marquis de. *See* l'Ausbespine, Charles de

Chasteauneuf, Monsieur de, 225

Chatham, Kent, 163, 314, 337, 339

Chaucer's tomb, Westminster Abbey, 193

Chauncy, Charles, 109, 110

Chaworth, George, Baron Chaworth of Tryme, 171, 174

Cheapside, London, 75, 319, 320, 346

Cheek, Sir Hatton, 15, 16

Cheese, 143

Cheke, Lady Essex, 185

Cheke, Sir Thomas, 185

Chelsea, London, 292

Chermont, France, 270

Cherries, 98

Chesapeake (Cissapeack), Virginia, 90, 91

Chester, Bishop of. *See* Morton, Thomas

Chevreuse, Duke de (Claude de Lorraine), 100, 101, 169, 254

Chevrieres-Miolans, Melchoir Mitte de, Marquis de St. Chaumont, 268

Chichester, Bishop of. *See* Montagu, Richard

Chickahominy, Virginia, 80

Chickahominy Indians, 60, 78

Chief Justice. *See* Coke, Sir Edward; Montagu, Sir Henry; Richardson, Sir Thomas

Chierasco: peace treaty signed at, 162

Chillingworth, William, 232, 235

Chimay, Prince of, 278

China: voyage to, 5

Chincheo. *See* Ch'uan-chou

Chinese, 6

Chomberg, Marshal de. *See* Schomberg, Henri de

Christenings: in Virginia, 66

Christian IV, King of Denmark, 7–9, 20, 21, 102, 110, 114, 117, 118, 132, 165, 166, 172, 245, 251, 254, 262, 286, 337, 339

Christina, Queen of Sweden, 188, 207, 217, 225, 239, 335, 338, 341, 344, 347

Christmas, 187–89, 192, 285, 289, 306, 310, 342, 347, 349, 350

Christopher, Marquis of Baden: killed, 266. *See also* Baden, Marquis of

Christ's College, Cambridge, 100, 133, 297

Chrysostom, St. John, 28, 29

Ch'uan-chou (Chincheo), Fukien Province, China, 5, 7

Church of England, 43, 135; Easter services in Paris, 157

Church union, 279

Cicero, 22, 297, 328

Civil War, 183, 276, 313

Clams (Slammes), 97

Clanricarde, Earl of, Richard. *See* Bourke, Richard

Clare, Sir Ralph, 127

Clare Hall, Cambridge, 223, 225, 226, 242

Clarkenwell, England, 277

Clermont, France, 162

Cleve, Duke of, 200

Clifford: finds concealed money, 143

Clifton, Catherine, Dowager Duchess of Lennox, 283, 286

Clinton, Theophilus, fourth Earl of Lincoln, 115, 116, 118

Cloth, 143, 155, 169

Clothing, 4, 74, 168, 273

Cná (red dye), 32

Cornwall, 250, 252, 331, 342, 349
Cornwallis, Anne, 267
Cornwallis, Charles, 348
Cornwallis, Frederick, 206, 209, 210, 346, 348
Coronation of Charles I, 203
Corpus Christi College, Cambridge, 208, 244, 245
Corpus Christi College, Oxford, 239
Cosin, the Rev. John, 132, 133
Cossacks, 238
Costumes, 3
Cottages, 216, 284
Cottington, Sir Francis, 129, 130, 135, 136, 142, 213, 214, 215, 306, 307, 309, 312, 318, 321, 342
Cotton, Sir Robert, 4, 101, 104, 114, 119, 148–50, 159, 163, 280, 282; letters to, 3, 5, 7, 16, 18
Cotton, Sir Thomas, 159, 163, 280, 282, 294
Council of Estate in Virginia. See Virginia, Council of
Council of War, 139
Counter (city prison), 334
Country men: not to live in London, 318, 320, 323, 330, 332, 348
Courteen (Curtyn), Sir William, 176, 178, 233, 236, 240, 285, 286, 290, 305
Courtenay, Sir William, 249, 252
Courtney: indicted for high treason, 249, 265
Courts, Superior: appealed to, 350
Cousin german, 50, 52
Cousins, Mr.: called into Star Chamber, 134
Coventry, Bishop of. See Morton, Thomas
Coventry, Sir Thomas, 124
Cowe, Sir Thomas, 28
Crabats (Croatians), 238, 281, 284, 333
Craddock, Herefordshire, 182, 183
Crane, Master of, 36
Cranfield, Lionel, Earl of Middlesex, 114, 115, 178, 206, 209, 254, 257, 313, 315
Craven, William, 118, 119, 178, 180, 203, 211, 225, 228, 229, 231, 238, 274, 281, 284
Crawley, Sir Francis, 306, 307
Cregney, Marshal, 182
Créqui, Marshal, 161
Creutznach, Germany, 204, 228, 229, 231, 234, 238, 256

Crewe, Sir Randolph, 43, 45, 78
Crime, unnatural, 158
Croatians. See Crabats
Crofts, James, 315, 317
Crofts, William, 127, 260, 263, 264, 312
Croke, Sir George, 146, 149, 265, 267
Cronenberg, Germany, 255
Crosbie, Sir Pierce, 172, 174
Crossbow, 36, 37
Crown, Clerk of, 326, 330
Croyden, Surrey, 74
Crucifix, 85, 205
Cruz-Sconse, 277, 285. See also Sconse
Crympen, Germany, 132
Cuba, 132
Cueva, Cardinal de, 278, 299, 301, 302
Curle (or Curll), Walter, Bishop of Bath and Wells, and Bishop of Winchester, 273, 276, 306, 307
Curtis (King's agent from Frankford), 338
Curtius, William, 342, 344
Curtyn, William. See Courteen, William
Customs: of farmers, 190, 191
Customs duties. See Tonnage and poundage
Cyprus, 247

D
Dabale: retreats, 290
Dalbier, John, 335, 337–40, 343
Dale, Lady Elizabeth, 63
Dale, Sir Thomas, 57, 62, 86, 87, 183
Dalham, Suffolk, 100, 102, 111
Dalton, Dorothy, 163
Dalton, Michael, 160, 163
Dalton, Sir Thomas, 16
Damariscotta River, Maine, 94
Damrells Cove, 93
Damyron, John, 83
Danby, Earl of. See Danvers, Henry
Dances, 3
Danish War (1625–29). See Thirty Years' War
Danube River, 229, 244, 246, 255, 266, 274
Danvers, Henry, Earl of Danby, 137, 138, 142, 160
Danzig, 188, 198, 261
Darcy, Elizabeth: marries Sir Thomas Savage, 109, 110
Darcy, Thomas, Earl Rivers, 110
Darnell, Sir Thomas, 120, 121
Darrell, Sir Marmaduke, 233, 236, 238

Fireworks, 8, 9, 292
Fish, 85, 90, 92, 93, 97; as fertilizer, 96
Fishhook, 330
Fishing, 223, 237, 305, 330, 346; off the coast of Scotland, 49, 305; in Canada, 83, 97; in Virginia, 93; in Massachusetts, 96, 97; in the North Sea, 118
Fitz Patrick, Laurence, 158, 160, 165, 166
Flanders, 104, 147, 169, 205, 217, 221, 251, 254, 278, 287, 289, 292, 301, 313, 322
Flatbottom boats. See Antwerp
Flax, 62, 79, 81, 86
Fleet: London, 112, 113, 117; Spanish, 113; Algiers, 143; New Spain, 132, 137; East India, 243
Fleetwood, Colonel George, 241, 245, 248, 269, 273
Fleetwood, Sir Miles, 206, 209
Fleming, Oliver, 224, 226
Flemish man of war, 74, 77, 78, 86
Flemmings, 98
Fletcher, John, 294
Flintshire, Wales, 314
Florence, 11, 12, 147, 268
Florence, Duke of, 253
Florentine agent, 179
Flowerdew, Temperance, 219
Flowerdieu Hundred, Virginia, 53
Flushing, 72
Flushing, Netherlands, 111, 269, 276
Fogg, Captain Richard, 139, 141
Foljambe, Sir Francis, 131, 133
Font of silver: gift to young Carnarvon, 339, 340
Fontainebleau, 161, 227
Fonteney, Monsieur de, 147
Force, Marshal de la, 150, 270, 291, 293, 346
Forcheim, Germany, 234
Forests. See Bois de Vincennes; Dean, Forest of; Durnighen, Forest of; Feckenham Forest; Gualtres, Forest of; Gillingham Forest; Sherwood Forest; Virginia, forests in
Fort: in Virginia, 80, 84
Foster: accompanies John Bassond to England, 293
Foster, the Rev. Christopher, 317
Foulis (Fowlis), Sir David, 147, 149
Fourde (minister): receives books, 29
Fowks: gets replevy from Court of Common Pleas, 134

Fowl, 90, 96
Foxe, Luke, 318, 319
France, 85, 117, 129, 194, 210, 217, 233, 253, 276, 281, 289, 323, 332; opposes Spain, 17; trades with Indians, 94
France, King of. See Louis XI; Louis XII; Louis XIII
France, Queen of. See Anne, Queen of France
Franciscans, 328
Franconia, 176, 324, 331
Frankendale, Germany, 194, 198, 201, 204, 221, 225, 229, 243, 289, 290, 303, 316, 333, 347
Frankford, Germany, 156, 175, 176, 177, 179, 181, 184, 187, 204, 205, 217, 218, 221, 222, 224, 225, 234, 245, 246, 251, 254, 256, 258, 262, 266, 267, 290, 303, 304, 309, 335, 337, 338, 342, 344; market, 239
Frederick V, King of Bohemia, 17, 18, 20, 21, 108, 116, 117, 136, 137, 164, 170, 176, 178, 179, 181, 183, 187, 198, 200, 203, 204, 211, 217, 218, 221, 225, 228, 229, 234, 238, 239, 243, 247, 270, 274, 275, 290, 291, 313, 316, 324, 325, 333, 335, 338, 340, 347, 348
Frederick Henry, Prince of Orange, 100, 161, 164, 167, 171–73, 176, 186, 195, 200, 207, 224, 244, 251, 254, 258, 267, 277, 278, 282, 287, 289, 290, 292, 296, 299, 302, 304, 309, 315, 322, 325, 333
Freewill, doctrine of, 141
Freistadt, Germany, 290
French church (Huguenot), 292, 308, 310
French Company, 214
French Morocco. See Salé; Muley Sydan
Frewen, Accepted, 205, 208
Friars: in the Low Countries, 328
Friesland, Netherlands, 222, 282
Frobisher, Martin, navigator, 50
Frost (of King's Chapel choir, Westminster Abbey), 190
Fryer, Archbishop Elector of, 258
Fuggers (firm of German merchants), 246
Fullers earth, 155
Fullerton, James, 144, 151, 153
Funerals and burials, 151, 159, 181, 190, 210, 213, 215, 257, 268, 273,

342, 343; in Virginia, 66. *See also* Embalming

Fyn Island, Denmark, 119

G

Gago: source of gold, 40

Galandrini, Caesar, 143, 144

Galas (ambassador of Ferdinand II), 162

Gallery of pictures: at the Louvre, 162

Gaming: to be punished in Virginia, 60, 61

Garaway (merchant), 32, 33

Garde des Sceaux, 162

Garnett, Thomas, 64

Gaston de France, Duc d'Orléans, 115, 161

Garway, Henry, 213, 214

Gatehouse, Tower of London, 46, 126, 136, 148, 203, 232, 323

Gates, Sir Thomas, 50, 51

Gaultres, Forest of, 114

Gayon, President (French Parliament), 162

Gazettes, 309, 312

Gelderland, Netherlands, 304. *See also* Guelders

Gell, Robert, 132, 133, 135, 138–40, 143

General grace, doctrine of, 141

General muster: in England and Wales to inventory arms, 207

General thanksgiving: for victory of Prince of Orange, 167

Generalissimo: rank resumed by Wallenstein, 243

Geneva, 17, 169

Genoa, Italy, 26, 273; Lantern of, 100

Gent (Gandt, Gaunt), Belgium, 172, 250, 251, 334. *See also* Sasse of Gaunt

George, 82, 84

Gerbier, Balthazar (the Duke's painter), 155, 158, 312, 315, 317, 333

Germans: skilled in mining sent to Virginia, 86; described as dull, 261

Germany, 132, 137, 156, 169, 170, 175, 176, 180, 184, 185, 188, 197, 201, 204, 211, 213, 217, 222, 243, 244, 248, 250–53, 262, 270, 271, 274, 278, 281, 289, 298, 302, 312, 322, 323, 328, 332, 342, 346, 349; States of, 193, 272

Gerrard, Anne: marries Dudley Carleton, 12

Gerrard, George, 12

Ghifford: brings letters from Germany, 227

Gibbes, Lieutenant (member of Virginia assembly), 53

Gibbs, John, 92, 94

Gibraltar. *See* Straits, The

Gifford: speaks against King of Sweden, 303

Gifford, Emanuel, 295, 297

Gifford, Gilbert, 187, 188, 196, 197, 199

Gifford, John, 257

Gifts: royal, 9, 105

Gill, Alexander, 129, 130, 232, 235

Gillingham Forest, 143, 144

Ginger, 161

Globe (theatre), 292

Globes: of silver, 247

Gloucestershire, 154, 157

Glover, Thomas, 9, 11

Gluckstadt, Germany, 132, 139, 286

Godfrey: slays Dodsworth, 265

Godfrey, William, 106, 107, 109

Gold, 143, 161, 176, 242, 247, 319, 321, 323, 338

Golde: guilty of high treason, 249

Golden Fleece, 269

Goldsmiths, 242, 268

Gondomar, Don Diego Sarmiento de Acunas, Condé de, 107, 108, 249, 252, 306

Gonville and Caius College, Cambridge, 2, 92, 307, 313

Gonzaga, Charles, Charles I, Duke of Mantua, 139, 141

Gonzuga: escapes after battle, 291

Goodman (English messenger to the King of Sweden), 156

Goodwin Sands (off the coast of Kent), 37

Gooseberries: in Massachusetts, 93, 98

Gordon, Sir Francis, 168, 260–63

Gore, John, 242, 245

Gore, Sir Thomas, 156

Gorges, Sir Ferdinando, 93, 94, 98, 137

Goring, Sir George, 38, 40, 50, 111, 199, 349

Goulston (Gulston), Dr. Theodore, 268, 271

Gourgainy (member of Virginia assembly), 53

Gout, 284, 295, 298

Graham, William, seventh Earl of Menteith, 165, 166

Hanau, Germany, 204, 304, 333
Hanaw, Earl of, 239
Hanger, George, 320, 322
Hanmer: marries maid of honor to queen, 192
Hansby, Ralph, 79, 80
Hanseatic League, 22
Hanstrudder, Sir Robert. *See* Anstruther, Sir Robert
Harcourt, Robert, 41
Harington, John, Lord Harington of Exton, 51
Harington, Lucy, Countess of Bedford, 4, 50, 51
Hariot, Thomas, 45, 325
Harlay, Jehan de, Marchioness of St. George, 111, 112
Harlem, Netherlands, 338, 340
Harrington, Sir James, 108
Harrington, Sarah, Lady La Zouche, 107, 108
Harrison, Ensign: in Virginia, 55
Harrison, John, 119, 120
Harsnett, Samuel, Archbishop of York, 146, 148, 296
Hart (Proctor of St. Gregory's Church), 205
Harvard College, 110
Harvey, Sir Francis, 306, 307
Harwick, 101, 102
Harwood, Colonel: slain before Maestricht, 287
Harwood, Sir Edward, 263, 264
Hassia, Germany, 259
Hasteville, David de: becomes Protestant, 308, 310
Hastings, Lady Dorothy, 4
Hastings, Henry, Earl of Huntington, 107, 108
Hatteville, David de. *See* Hasteville, David de
Hatton, Sir Christopher, 35
Hatton, Elizabeth, 34, 50
Hatton House, 34, 184
Hausted, Peter, *The Rival Friends*, 235
Havana, 233
Havana Montanca, Cuba, 132
Hay, James, first Earl of Carlisle, and Viscount Doncaster, 4, 42, 43, 45, 117, 129, 142, 146, 151, 165, 168, 179, 197, 199, 209, 237, 239, 240, 259, 273, 275
Hay, Lucy, Countess of Carlisle, 106, 108
Healing: king's gift, 47; by an old

woman, 269. *See also* Doctors and physicians; Surgeons
Heath, Sir Robert, 46, 47, 203, 205, 206, 209, 264, 297; attorney general, 160
Hector, in *Aeneid*, 215
Heidelberg, Germany, 20, 184, 198, 204, 218, 222, 225, 229, 243, 288, 289, 296, 303, 348
Heins, Peter, 137, 233,
Heinsius, Daniel, 258, 260
Helen, 169
Hemp, 62, 81, 86
Henri, Duc de Rohan. *See* Rohan, Henri
Henrico, Virginia, 52, 67
Henrietta Maria, Queen of England, 100, 101, 105, 106, 108, 114, 118, 127, 139, 142, 172, 183, 192, 212, 216, 219, 223, 227, 228, 232, 264, 266, 270, 272, 280, 284, 289, 292, 294, 297, 300, 305, 307, 310, 312, 321, 334, 337, 340; Queen's portion, 114, 151, 169, 184, 187, 197, 217, 220, 233, 242
Henriette (island in the West Indies), 152
Henry III, king of England, 348
Henry III, king of France, 102
Henry IV, king of France, 11, 188, 196, 308; death of, 21, 22
Henry VIII, king of England, 164, 189, 291, 294, 296, 348; statute of, 13
Henry Frederick, Prince of Wales, 3, 5, 7, 15, 16, 126, 252, 282; untimely death, 25
Hepburn, Sir John, 246, 248
Heralds, 191, 231, 348. *See also* Pursuivants
Herbert, Edward, Baron Herbert of Chirbury of Castle Island, 215, 218, 268, 271
Herbert, Sir Henry, 194, 196
Herbert, Philip, Earl of Montgomery and Earl of Pembroke, 3, 4, 107, 108, 154, 158, 260, 349, 351; Lord Chamberlain, 257
Herbert, Sir William, third Earl of Pembroke, Baron Powis, 107, 108, 223, 224, 226, 271
Hereford, Herefordshire, 289, 345
Herefordshire, 182
Herne, Sir Edward, 132, 133
Herrick, Robert, 108
Herring (fish), 96, 305; fleet, 152
Hertford (Hartford), Hertfordshire, 155

Manners, Francis, sixth Earl of Rutland, 110–12, 134, 136, 153, 199, 265, 267

Manners, Lady Katherine, Duchess of Buckingham, 106, 108, 267

Mannourié (physician), 43, 45

Mannsell, Sir Robert, 9, 11, 313–15

Mansfeldt, Count Ernest de, 100, 102, 114, 140, 267, 302, 335, 337, 341

Mantua, Duchy of, 147

Manuscript: binding of, 32

Manuscripts: of Sir Edward Coke, 249

Manwaring, Roger, 124, 125

Manwood, Sir Peter, 37, 38

Maps: brought by Prince of Piedmont, 24

Marbury (Master of one of the *Lion's Whelps*), 139

Marchant of London, 83, 87

Marchpane, 115

Mareuil, M. de Fontenay, 230

Margate, Kent, 36, 37

Marigolde, 77

Marillac, Michel de, 233, 236, 270

Mariners: demand wages, 112; contract with, 350

Markham, Robert, 89, 91

Marmaduke, 94

Marriages: in Virginia, 66, 67, 89, 90

Marseilles, 153

Marshalsea Prison, London, 143, 206, 210, 269

Marsham, Robin, 217, 221, 229, 281, 283

Martha's Vineyard, Massachusetts, 98

Martin, Henry, 168, 170, 349, 350

Martin, Captain John, 59, 64; Martin-Brandon (plantation), 52; Martin's Hundred (plantation), 53, 63, 69, 80; order concerning, 53, 55, 56; assembly examines his patient, 54, 55; exemptions, 60

Martin, Richard, 44–46, 49

Mary, daughter of Charles I (afterwards Princess of Orange): governess appointed for, 1631, 177, 306

Mary, Princess and Queen, 151, 159, 191, 192

Mary Magdalene: picture of, 205

Maryland, 90

Mason, Robert, 310, 311

Masques, 3, 152, 185, 186, 197, 199, 239, 322

Mass, 224, 265, 285

Massachusetts, 92, 93, 95, 96–99, passim

Massacre of Ambonia, 158

Massacre of 1622 in Virginia, 78

Master of the Rolls, 295, 297, 343

Mastiff, 65, 277

Masts: for ships, 318, 320

Mathematical instruments: Raleigh's, 46

Mattaponi River, Virginia, 89, 91

Matthew, Sir Tobie, 240

Matthias, Emperor of Germany and King of Bohemia (1612–19), 20, 22

Maurice, Prince of Nassau, 22, 92, 94, 135, 169

Mauritania, West Africa, 41

Maximilian, Duke of Bavaria, 20, 22, 246

Maxwell, James, 219, 338, 339

Maxwell, Robert, 339

Maycock, Samuel, 70

Mayerne, Sir Theodore Turquet de, 285, 289, 291

Mazarin, Giulio, 115, 149, 150

Maze River. *See* Maas River

Mead, the Rev. Joseph, 100, 101; letters to, 99, 104, 108, 111, 113, 115, 116, 118, 119, 120, 121, 122, 124, 125, 127, 128, 131, 133, 136, 139, 141, 144, 145, 149, 150; writes to Sir Martin Stuteville, 101

Meal, 334, 337; chandlers, 155

Mechlin, Archbishop of, 279, 350

Mechlin, Belgium, 296, 299, 301

Mecklenburg, Duke of. *See* Adolphus Frederick I

Medici, Cosimo de, II, Grand Duke of Tuscany, 11, 12

Medici, Marie de, 17, 21, 22, 167, 181, 183, 184, 187, 196, 201, 225, 254, 272, 304, 306, 308, 311, 316, 324, 334, 337, 340, 342

Meek, William: marries Elizabeth Scudamore, 185

Meldram (Scottish prisoner), 165

Melium, Germany, 269

Melton: robbed and slain, 138

Melvin (Scottish prisoner), 126

Men: to be sent to occupy land of Virginia Company, 57

Mennes, John, 140, 141

Menteith (Montyth) Earl of. *See* Graham, William

Mentz, 181, 186, 187, 194, 204, 210, 217, 218, 221, 228, 229, 243, 256, 259, 333, 335, 338, 348

Mentz, Archduke, of, 229

Merchants, 5, 117, 134, 151, 155, 175, 201, 223; adventurers, 35, 139, 202, 253, 297, 338, 341; foreign, 120; Dutch, 175; English, 175, 228, 233; Canadian, 217, 220; Transylvanian, 262; at Delft, 340, 343

Merode, Count de, 255

Merton College, Oxford, 38, 271

Mesitz, Germany, 184

Messene, Sicily, 180, 182

Metz, France, 267, 342

Meuse River. See Maas River

Mexico, Bay of, 269

Michelbourne, Sir Edward, 5, 6, 10

Middlesborough, Yorkshire, 36–39, 74, 276

Middlesex, Earl of. See Cranfield, Lionel

Milan, 180, 211, 224

Milan, Archbishop of, 259

Millefleur (near Turin), Italy, 24, 26

Milton, John, 158, 254, 257

Minden, Germany, 182

Mines, 86, 245

Minister: use of the word, 128

Minos (mythological Greek judge), 32

Mint, chief officer of, 113

Misselden, Edward, 200, 202

Mitre Tavern: in Fleet Street, 181, 183. See also Tavern, in Fleet Street

Moinvick (fort in Germany), 194

Mole (or Molle), John, 11, 12

Molina, Nicola, 3, 5

Moll, Estinien, 88

Monbazon, Madame de: cause of fight at court, 169

Mouceaux: site of French Court in Paris, 169

Money, out of Spain: for Archduchess Isabella, 312, 314, 327

Monhaccke (Indian tribe of man-eaters), 99

Monies: scarce in England, 49

Monks: in the Low Countries, 328

Monopolies: granted, 261

Monsieur. See Orléans, Duc d'

Monson, Sir William, 346, 348

Montagu, Sir Charles, 35

Montagu, Edward, Viscount Mandeville and Earl of Manchester, 185, 186

Montagu, Sir Henry, Earl of Manchester and Viscount Mandeville, 158, 178; Chief Justice, 42, 44, 46, 47, 264; Keeper of the Privy Seal, 154, 179, 213, 261, 268, 280, 306, 309, 312, 313, 315, 318, 321, 343, 350

Montagu, Richard, Bishop of Chichester, 134, 135, 140–42

Montagu, Walter, 114, 115, 118, 215, 292, 294, 310, 312, 315, 318, 321

Montagu-Douglas-Scott, Walter John, Duke of Buccleuch, 13

Montaigne, George, Archbishop of York, 135, 136

Montanca, Cuba, 132

Montargis, France, 293

Montauban, France, 311

Montecucculi, Count Raimund, 289

Montferrat, Italy, 147, 150

Montgomery, Countess of. See Vere Susan De

Montgomery, Earl of. See Herbert, Philip

Montmorency, Duke de, Henri II, 169, 282, 291, 293, 296, 299, 302, 306, 311, 316, 324, 327, 346; beheaded, 323, 331

Montpellier, Bishop of, 311

Montpellier, France, 311

Moone, 9

Moorefields (London park), 327, 329

Moorgate, London, 273

Moors: inhabit Salé, 119

Moravia, Baron of, 164

Moravia, Czechoslovakia, 164, 175, 195, 198, 200, 321, 324

More, [Henry?] (a Jesuit), 137–39, 143

Morgan, General Sir Charles, 99, 100, 139, 141, 174, 276

Moroccan ambassador (1600), 1

Morocco, Sultan of. See Sydan, Muley

Morton, Earl of. See Douglas, William

Morton, Peter, 153, 154

Morton, Thomas, Bishop of Chester, Lichfield, and Durham, 273, 276, 282, 283

Moselle River, 217, 221, 222, 225, 234, 243, 256, 258, 279

Mosquitoes, 86

Moulins, France, 306

Mourning: at court for kings of Sweden and Bohemia, 338, 340

Moutapass (Indian name of Robert Markham), 89

Mulberry trees, 62, 85

Muley Hamet, Sultan of Barbary, 1

Muley Sydan, Sultan of Morocco, 119

Mulheim, Germany, 20, 21

Munich, 242, 250, 251, 259, 263, 266, 274, 284, 285

Münster, 182, 245

Murad IV, Sultan of Turkey, 248

Powhatan (Indian chief in Virginia), 78, 90, 91
Powis, Lord. *See* Herbert, Sir William
Prague, 20, 21, 179, 181, 198, 201, 204, 227, 281, 284
Pratt, Henry, 181, 183
Pratt, Sheriff: loses election, 280
Prayer: in Virginia Assembly, 53; for newswriters, 312, 314, 317
Precedents (presidents), 13, 113, 122
Predestination, 141
Prefines, 14
Pregnotaries, 318, 320
Prerogatives, 15, 123, 125; royal, 115
President of the North. *See* Wentworth, Sir Thomas
Preston, Elizabeth, 139
Preston, Richard, Lord Dingwall and Earl of Desmond, 48, 50, 138, 143
Preston, Thomas, 106, 107
Price, Dr. Theodore, 190, 192
Prices: of food, 155
Priest: use of the word, 128
Prim, Captain (of the East India fleet), 39
Primerose, Gilbert, 310
Prinaquie River, New England, 93
Le Prince, by Blazac, 214, 215
Prince Hendrick River (Dutch name of Kennebec River), Maine, 92–93
Princeland, Ile of, Netherlands, 172
Printers and printing, 18, 144, 261, 309, 312. *See also* Butter, Nathaniel
Prisoners: pardoned, 344
Prisons. *See* Counter; Gatehouse; Marshalsea; Newgate
Privy Council, 203, 334, 348
Privy counsellors, 160
Privy Seal, Keeper of. *See* Howard, Henry; Montagu, Henry
Profane speech: called into question, 330
Prohibitions: rulings on, 349; debated, 350
Prosperous, 77
Protestants' church, 200, 268
Provence, France, 153, 169
Prussia, 269, 273
Prynne, William, 349, 351
Puckering, Sir Thomas, 152, 153, 157, 166, 173, 178, 282, 286, 291, 313; letters to, 151, 154, 159, 163, 167, 170, 174, 179, 186, 196, 202, 215, 294, 346, 348
Puget: lends money to Marie de Medici, 23

Pulauren (Puylauren) [young animal]: Monsieur flees from Paris with, 328, 331
Pulo Candcnor, Ile of, Cambodia, 5
Purchase, 7
Puritans, 118, 131, 133, 148, 263, 306, 310
Pursuivants, 250, 303. *See also* Heralds
Purveyance, 14
Pye, Walter, 276, 279
Pyne, Arthur, 252
Pyne, William, 252
Pyrrhus, King, 214

Q
Quebec, 151, 153, 217, 219, 220, 242, 243, 245
Queen of Poland. *See* Constance of Styria
Queen Mother. *See* Medici, Marie de
Queen's College, Cambridge, 104, 192, 193, 232, 241, 244, 245
Queen's portion. *See* Henrietta Maria
Quester, Matthew De, 252, 253

R
Racouski, Joannes Albertus, 167, 168
Radcliffe, George, 326, 328, 330
Radcliffe, Robert Earl of Sussex, 3, 5
Ragotzi, Prince of Transylvania, 204, 259, 262, 270, 321, 324
Rain, Bavaria, 284; castle of, 255, 281, 309, 319, 321
Rainton, Sir Nicholas, 272, 306
Raleigh, Carew, 48
Raleigh, Lady Elizabeth, 46, 48
Raleigh, Sir Walter, 5, 37, 40–42, 44–47, 50, 110, 264, 325
Rammekens, Fort, Holland, 36, 37
Ramsey (Quartermaster to Marquis Hamilton), 229
Ramsey, David, 177, 184, 186, 191, 197, 199, 200, 202, 209, 213, 215, 219, 229, 243, 245, 261, 265, 271, 277, 305
Rand (Master of the *Jonathan*), 83
Randolph, Thomas, *The Jealous Lovers*, 235
Rankin, Archibald, 171, 242
Rape (crime), 166, 310
Rape-mills, 237
Raspberries, 93, 94, 98
Rastell, Thomas, 301, 302
Ratisbon. *See* Regensburgh
Raven, John, 137, 138
Raynborowe, William, 133

Rohan, Benjamin de, Seigneur de
Soubise, 101, 102, 104, 128, 130, 139
Rohan, Henri, Duc de Rohan, 128, 130,
139, 173, 213, 215
Rolfe, John, 64, 70
Roman Catholics, 199, 205, 265; death
of three, 249, 253; abbot becomes
Protestant, 308, 310. *See also* Papists;
Recusants
Romanov, Michael, Emperor of Russia,
39, 41, 273
Romans, King of. *See* Sweden, King of
Romberg, Count, 293
Rome, 85, 169, 188, 195, 205, 206,
251, 301
Roos, Lord. *See* Cecil, William, Lord
Roos
Rosicrusians (Rosy Cross), 116, 117
Rosse, England, 189, 231
Rossingham, Ensign Edward, 53, 56
Rostock, Germany, 172
Rosy Cross. *See* Rosicrusians
Rothenburg, Germany, 180
Rotherfield Greys, Oxford, 273, 276
Rotterdam, 20
Rouen, Duke of, 346
Rouen, France, 149, 157, 169, 308
Rowe, Captain John, 139, 141
Roxas, François de, Duke of Lerma,
167, 170
Roxburgh, Lord of. *See* Ker, Robert
Royal James, 39
Royal Library: in Paris, 17
Royal prerogative, 115
Royston, Yorkshire, 216, 219, 232
Rubens, Peter, 195
Rudolf II, Holy Roman Emperor, 246
Rudyerd, Sir Benjamin, 122, 124
Ruggle, George: author of "Ig-
noramus," 225
Rusignan: surrenders, 150
Russell, Anne: marries George Digby,
113
Russell, Edward, third Earl of Bedford,
51, 113
Russell, Francis, fourth Earl of Bedford,
135, 136, 147, 148, 240, 287, 288,
334, 336
Russell, Margaret: marries James Hay,
237, 240
Russell, Sir William, 258, 260
Russell Island, Chesapeake Bay, 89, 91
Russia, 39, 40, 248. *See also* Muscovy;
Romanov, Michael
Russia, Emperor of. *See* Romanov,
Michael

Rutland, Countess. *See* Sidney, Elisabeth
Rutland, Earl of. *See* Manners, Francis
Ryder, William, 16, 17

S
Sabbath, 67
Sackville, Mistress C. (masquer), 4
Sackville, Edward, fourth Earl of Dor-
set, 117, 141, 143, 159, 249, 252,
306
Sackville, Richard, third Earl of Dorset,
17, 18
Saddles, 312, 315
Saffron, 237
Sagadahoc (Kennebec) River, Maine, 92
Sailors: demand wages, 112
St. Alban Hall, Oxford, 193
St. Andrew, 129, 130
St. Andrews University, Scotland, 282
St. Angelo (castle), Italy, 195
St. Anthony's fire (erysipelas), 281
St. Bartholomew's, London, 181
St. Chaumont, Marquis de: French am-
bassador, 230, 266, 270, 272
St. Christopher's Island, West Indies,
237, 242
St. Claude, 140
St. Cross Hospital, Winchester, 190,
192
St. David's, Wales, Bishop of. *See* Field,
Theophilus
St. Denys, 305
St. George: surrenders, 150
St. Giles in the Fields, London, 124, 261
St. Gregory's Church (beside St. Paul's),
London, 205, 208
St. James's, London, 106, 109, 193,
282, 306, 321
St. James's Park, London, 105
St. John, Beauchamp, 118, 119
St. John, Dorothy: marries Edward
Bourchier, Earl of Bath, 289, 291
St. John, Sir Oliver, Earl of Bolinbroke,
16, 18, 115, 116, 291
St. John's College, Cambridge, 244;
library, 327, 329
St. Katherines, London, 269
St. Martin's: ordnance shipped from,
126
St. Marys, Oxford, 91, 312, 314
St. Omer, France, 232, 301; College,
303
St. Paul's Cathedral, 75, 192, 205, 208,
210, 226, 237, 242, 245, 248, 253,
257, 266, 272, 273, 295, 297, 298,
300, 306, 326

St. Quentin, France, 293, 299
St. Rauy, Monsieur de (King Charles's huntsman), 304
St. Romuald, French Order of, 308
St. Stephen's, near Canterbury, 38
St. Stephen's Day (December 26), 184
Salazar, Count of: hanged in effigy, 278
Salé, (Sallee), French Morocco, 119, 120
Salisbury, Earl of. *See* Cecil, William
Salisbury, Wiltshire, 101; court at, 143
Salisbury House, London, 136, 236, 273
Salmon, 96
Salt, 85, 88, 322
Salutes: from guns, 7, 8, 21
Salvador, Brazil, 159, 163
Sampson, 131
Sanderson, William, 241, 244
Sandwich: speaks foul words at Whitehall, 216, 219, 220
Sandy Point, Virginia, 82
Sandys, Sir Edwin, 78, 95, 119, 188; letters to, 75, 79, 80, 83, 87
Santa Cruz, Marquis of. *See* Bazan, Alvaro de
San Tomé, Venezuela, 43
Sasquasahanacks (Indians), 99
Sassafras, 63, 98
Sasse of Gaunt (fort), 289
Savage, Sir Arthur, 237
Savage, Thomas (Indian interpreter), 88–90
Savage, Thomas, Viscount, 110, 111, 154, 158
Savages, 89, 95, 243. *See also* Indians
Savile, Sir Henry, Provost of Eaton, 12, 37, 38
Savile, Sir Thomas, 113, 114
Savoy, Duke of. *See* Charles Emmanuel I; Victor Amadeus I
Savoy, France, 273, 300
Savoy, London, 210
Sawmills, 237
Saxe Coburg, Duke of: seeks aid to defend Coburg, 319, 321
Saxe Weimar, Bernard, Duke of, 239, 247, 256, 259, 285, 313, 316, 319, 321, 328, 331, 335, 337, 338, 344
Saxe Weimar, Ernest I, Duke of, 153, 154, 224
Saxe Weimar, William, Duke of, 299
Saxony, Elector of. *See* John George I
Saxony, Germany, 184, 254, 284, 302, 313, 316, 319, 321, 325; King of, 263
Scaglia, Abbot of, 168, 170, 172

Scharnuste (French ambassador to Sweden), 210
Schelde River, Belgium, 277, 289
Scholer (tutor to sons of Queen of Bohemia), 341
Schomberg, Count Henri de, 149, 150, 161, 163
Schorndorf, Germany, 212
Schweinfurt (Swinford), Germany, 324, 331
Scipieres, Count de: Master of Horse to Queen Henrietta Maria, 106
Sconse (skonce; shenks-sconce) [harbor fortifications], 102, 161, 277, 285, 347
Scotch-Irish. *See* Irish Scot
Scotland, 177, 184, 186, 191, 193, 196, 213, 216, 226, 295, 297, 305, 318, 320, 338, 340, 349; Lord President of, 165
Scots, 128
Scott, Walter, Earl of Baccleuch, 194, 196
Scottish news, 119
Scottishmen: Council of Duke of Buckingham, 126
Scrivener, 155
Scrofula. *See* King's evil
Scudamore, Elizabeth, 183, 185
Scudamore, John, 182, 239; letters to, 181, 183, 189, 190, 193, 199, 205, 209, 213, 219, 223, 226, 231, 236, 241, 245, 249, 253, 257, 260, 265, 268, 272, 276, 279, 283, 286, 288, 292, 297, 300, 303, 305, 308, 314, 320, 323, 329, 332, 334, 339, 345
Sculembach: taken prisoner, 302
Sea instruments: Raleigh's, 46
Secretary of Estate: in Virginia, 50, 53, 65, 66, 73
Sedley (Sidley), Elizabeth, 37, 38
Sedley (Sidley), Sir John, 38
Selden, John, 184, 187, 188, 202, 232, 234
Seneca, Marcus Annaeus: quoted, 16, 78
Senegal River, West Africa, 40, 41
Serjeants' Inn, London, 343
Sermons: by Roger Manwaring recanted, 124, 125
Servants: gifts to, 9; French, 105, 106, 109, 111; Polish, 262; beheaded by Louis XIII, 311, 316
Servants in Virginia, 64; not to be enticed away, 62; female, marriage contract required, 67; as wealth, 74

250, 251, 252, 254–56, 258, 260, 262, 266, 271, 272, 324
Timber: in Virginia, 85, 93
Timbucktu, West Africa, 40, 41
Tin mines: in Cornwall, 349
Tirol, Austria, 260
Tisquanto (Indian servant of Sir Ferdinando Gorges), 98, 99
Tobacco, 63, 73, 80, 81, 155, 161; price of, 58; shops, 261
Tod, Otto, 259, 262
Toledo, Cardinal of, 288, 300, 314
Tonnage and poundage, 125, 126, 131, 235, 280
Toothache, 268
Torgau, Germany, 328, 331, 333, 335
Torsonny, Prince of: taken prisoner, 171
Touchet, Ferdinando, Lord Audley, 249, 252, 253. *See also* Tuchet
Toulouse, France, 323, 327, 331
Tounson, Dr. Robert, Dean of Westminster and Bishop of Salisbury, 43, 45
Touraine, France, 316
Tours, France, 311
Tower Hill, 163
Tower of London, 45, 46, 116, 119, 121, 127, 145, 148, 160, 178, 191–93, 200, 203, 206, 207, 209, 231, 234, 240, 242, 266, 277, 301, 306, 310, 325, 326, 329, 334, 342, 344
Townley, Zouch, 129, 130
Townsend, Aurelian, 4, 186, 197, 199, 201
Trade: with China, 5; in Virginia, 59, 67
Transylvania, 321
Trarbach (Torbach), now Traben-Trarbach, Germany, 234
Travel: in Virginia restricted, 65
Treason, 126
Treasurer. *See* Cecil, Sir Robert; Ley, Sir James; Weston, Richard
Treasurer, 72, 75, 76
Treaties: between France and England, 142; of St. Germain, 153; of Henry IV, 243; at Maestricht, 309
Tredescant, John, 318–20
Treenail, 237, 239
Trees: in New England, 93
Tremouille, Duchess of. *See* Brabantine, Charlotte
Trent River, England, 154
Trepan, 273
Trevor, Sir Sackville, 313–15

Triall, 84, 87
Triers, Elector of: fortresses of, 278, 346
Triers, Germany, 221, 222, 234
Trinity College, Cambridge, 16, 109, 110, 173, 174, 209, 230, 232, 238, 241, 248, 257
Trinity College, Dublin, 153
Trinity College, Oxford, 235
Trinity House, London, 313, 315
Triumph, 305
Troppau (Truppa), now Opava, Czechoslovakia, 164
Truce of fourteen days: in Germany between Protestants and Catholics, 217, 222
Tuchet, Mervyn, Earl of Castlehaven, 154, 158, 160, 163, 165, 166. *See also* Touchet
Tucker, Captain William, 52, 56
Tufton, Cecily: marries Francis Manners, sixth Earl of Rutland, 109, 110
Tufton, Sir John, 110
Tunbridge, Kent, 210, 212, 213, 215, 218
Turin, Italy, 26, 154, 208, 268, 275, 283, 286
Turkey: ambassador to, 29, 300; compared to Virginia, 74; military affairs in, 247
Turkey, trading company, 134
Turkey, Sultan of. *See* Osman I
Turkeys, 98
Turkish Chiaus (messenger), 47, 49
Turkish men of war, 312, 315, 327
Turks, 20, 21, 23, 239, 253, 312
Turner, Dr. Samuel, 120, 121
Turner, Thomas, 314, 317
Tuscany, Duchess dowager of: dies, 192
Tuscany, Grand Duke of. *See* Medici, Cosimo de, II
Tuscany, Italy, 316
Tuttlefields, London, 213, 229, 261
Twine, John, 53
Twisse, William, 228, 231
Tyburn, London, 106, 107, 136, 166
Tyrret, Robert, 131

U
Uladislaus. *See* Ladislas IV
Ulm (Ohme), Germany, 180, 217, 221, 229, 244
Unicorn horns, 318, 320
University: to be erected in Virginia, 58
Upnor Castle, Kent, 7, 10
Urban VIII, 177, 195, 196, 206, 233, 239, 251–52, 258, 259, 323

Westmoreland, Earl of. *See* Fane, Mildmay

Weston, Anne: marries Basil Feilding, second Earl of Denbigh, 138, 302

Weston, Jerome, second Earl of Portland, 208, 245, 248, 266, 268, 273, 275, 287, 293, 305, 312, 315

Weston, Richard, first Earl of Portland, 99, 100, 136, 138, 160, 173, 183, 257, 302; Lord Treasurer, 163, 179, 181, 184, 191, 192, 203, 206, 210, 224, 253, 258, 315, 318, 320, 321, 350

Westphalia, Germany, 177, 182

Weyanoke, Virginia, 80

Weybridge (Waybridge) Park, Huntingdonshire, 154

Wheat, 73

Whelps, 312, 315

Whetstone, Captain: erroneously reported dead, 276

Whitaker, Jabez, 79

White, Francis, Bishop of Carlisle, of Norwich, and of Ely, 347, 348

Whitehall, 4, 40–42, 44, 45, 49, 107, 116, 131, 141, 142, 154, 163, 167, 182, 199, 203, 216, 219, 236, 257, 275, 279, 289, 294, 307, 316, 318, 346, 348. *See also* Banqueting House; Cockpit

Whitelocke, Sir James, 280, 283, 306

"Wicked Bible," 261

Wickham, William, 70

Wilcock, Captain: plantation at Accomack, Virginia, 88

Wilcocks (servant of John Scudamore), 279

Wilcox, Rowlande, 339, 341

Wilcox, Thomas, 341

Willemstadt, Netherlands, 172

William, 142

Williams, Sir Abraham, 168, 255, 257, 266, 267, 280

Williams, John, Bishop of Lincoln, 159, 163, 192, 216, 220, 238, 240, 266, 315, 318, 323, 326, 327, 329, 349

Williams, Sir Roger, *The Actions of the Lowe Countries*, 38

Wilson, Sir Thomas, 40, 41, 46

Wilton, Wiltshire, 101

Wiltshire, 145

Wimbledon, Viscount. *See* Cecil, Edward

Winchester, 190, 192, 215, 216, 295, 297; Bishopric of, 213

Winchester, Bishop of. *See* Curle, Walter; Neile, Richard

Winchester, Marquis of. *See* Paulet, John

Windebank, Francis, 277, 279, 280, 309, 312, 313, 318, 321

Windmill Hill, London, 7

Windsor, 37, 91, 249, 318

Wines: Canary, 81; in Virginia, 98; customs collected on, 254

Wingfield, Sir James, 177, 178

Wingfield, Richard, 178

Wingfield family, 158

Winten [Weiden?] (near Nuremberg), Germany, 244

Winwood, Sir Ralph, 15, 34; letter to, 13

Wismar, Germany, 188

Withipole, Sir William, 34, 35

Witten, Grave: succeeds Count Ernest of Nassau as deputy marshal of the field, 282

Wittenberg, Germany, 170, 171, 174, 346

Wolfenbuttel, Germany, 207, 217, 221, 251, 313, 321, 325

Wolgast, Germany, 169, 172

Wolstenholme, Sir John, 237, 240

Woman: burned at Smithfield, 250

Wood Street, London, 192

Woodbridge, Suffolk, 160

Wool, 101

Worcester, Earl of. *See* Somerset, Edward; Somerset, Henry

Worcestershire, 253, 256

Worms, Germany, 194, 267

Wornitz (Wormlits) River, Germany, 246

Wortley, Sir Francis, 113, 114

Wren, Matthew, Dean of Windsor, 193, 196

Wrestling: prohibited in London, 329

Wright, John, 326, 330, 331

Wright, Robert, Bishop of Bristol, 306, 307

Wriothesley, Henry, third Earl of Southampton, 50, 51, 90, 103; letters to, 88, 95

Wurtemberg, Duke of. *See* Eberhard III

Wurtzburg, Bishop of: ambassador to France, 217, 221

Wyatt, Sir Francis, 90, 91, 94; letter to, 92

Wyatt's Rebellion (1554), 192

Y

Yale, Sir Robert, 152
Yarmouth, Norfolk, 223, 286, 303, 305,
    330
Yarrows Ordinary, London, 265
Yeardley, Sir George, Governor of Vir-
    ginia, 40, 41, 50, 52–54, 56, 59, 63,
    70, 72, 74, 76–78, 80–82, 85–88,
    95, 103, 104, 219
Yeardley, Ralph, 74, 75, 82
Yelverton, Charles, 328
Yelverton, Sir Christopher, 192, 193,
    328
Yelverton, Sir Henry, 34, 35, 42, 44
Yelverton, Robert, 193
Yeworth (a solicitor of Oxfordshire),
    160
York, 165, 254; council at, 232
York, Archbishop of. *See* Harsnett,
    Samuel; Neile, Richard; Montaigne,
    George
York, President of. *See* Wentworth,
    Thomas
York Herald, 348
York House, 158
Yorkshire, 36, 113, 334
Young, Patrick, 280, 282
Ypres, Belgium, 278

Z

Zeeland, Netherlands, 230, 254, 287,
    289, 292, 304, 316
Zierikzee (Zuricksea), Netherlands, 289
Zouch, Edward La, Baron Zouche, 48,
    49, 108
Zurat. *See* Surat, India
Zwickau (Swickaw), Germany, 344